Meeting

the

Mystery

MEETING the MYSTERY

*Exploring the Aware Presence
At the Heart of All Life*

NIRMALA

Endless Satsang Foundation

http://endless-satsang.com

Copyright © 2012 by Daniel Erway (aka Nirmala)

ISBN: 9781468155693

Cover photo: © Jim Hughes / Dreamstime.com

All rights reserved. No part of this book may be used or reproduced by any means, graphic, electronic, or mechanical, including photocopying, recording, taping, or by any information storage retrieval system without the written permission of the publisher except in the case of brief quotations embodied in critical articles and reviews.

Contents

Introduction ix

CHAPTER 1: AWARENESS 1

Awareness Is Never the Same Way Twice—We Are All Baby Ducks—Sensing Awareness—Becoming More Aware of Your Ribs—Life as a Sitcom—Fears Are True, but Fortunately Not Very True—Is There One or Many? Yes!—Be Curious About What Is—The Qualities of Awareness (Mp3 recording)

CHAPTER 2: SPACE 27

What Is Found in Lack?—Self-Inquiry —Become a Lake—Giving Space to Everything—Pointers for Giving Space—Emptiness Knows Better Than You—You Cannot Be Harmed—Awareness Is Limitless (Mp3 recording)

CHAPTER 3: WISDOM 51

The Heart's Wisdom—The Contracted Heart—The Heart's Wisdom in Relationships—The Beginning That Never Happened to the End That Never Comes—The Truth Has Got a Hold of Us—Inner vs. Outer Guidance—Letting Small Truths Be Small—Decisions Are Not That Important—Our Inner Compass Is Always Working—The Radio of the Mind—True Healing—Less Than Half Isn't Nothing! —The Experiential Qualities of Truth (Mp3 recording)

CHAPTER 4: DESIRE AND SUFFERING   81

Desiring What Is—Surrender Is What Is—Following Desire Back to Its Source—The Gift Life Is Delivering to Your Door—Suffering Is a Patient Teacher— The Mother of All Habits—Half of the Truth—When the Heart Tastes Emptiness, It Is Very Full— Is the Sky Really Blue? —Rejection and Desire vs. Love (Mp3 recording)

CHAPTER 5: REALITY AND BELIEFS   115

Is the Brain the Source of Consciousness?—Who Is There to Do Something?—What Do I Do When There Is No Doer?—What Happens When We Die?—No One Has Ever Spoken the Whole Truth—Now You See the Ego, and Now You Don't—The Spectrum of Being and Doing—Slaying the Dragons of Our Core Beliefs—The Game of Believing—"Why?" and "Why Not?" Cancel Each Other Out—What Is Real (Mp3 recording)

CHAPTER 6: DAILY LIFE   153

Pulled in Two Directions—Tell the Superego to Shut Up—Negative Feelings Are Doorways to Essence—Life Is a One-Room Schoolhouse—Motivation After Spiritual Awakening—Guilt Is Not Very Useful Nor Meaningful—The Ego Is a Pimp—Leaving or Staying When You Get Contracted—Defending vs. Acceptance—Letting Sexual Energy Be Bigger Than Your Body—Drowning Your Fear in Love—Seeing Love in Every Action—Authenticity and Love—The Truth in Daily Life (Mp3 recording)

CHAPTER 7: GRACE   189

Invitation to Rest—The Flower of Awakening—Grace Is All There Is—Staying Awake Until Grace Comes—The Point of Spiritual Practice (Mp3 recording)

Appendix 1: Beyond No Self   205
Appendix 2: Love Is for Giving   217
About the Author   225

Introduction

Life is a profound mystery. What is the source of the aliveness and awareness, which are fundamental to all life? What is the nature of desire, and how do our desires relate to suffering? How do we know what is true? What is the nature of belief, and how do our beliefs affect our ability to experience the deeper reality that is always here? And in the midst of these mysteries, how do we live our daily lives in the most satisfying and integrated way?

Although there are no final answers to these questions, we can endlessly explore them and discover new dimensions and possibilities in our lives and in our spiritual evolution. Every insight and new perspective adds to our realization of the truth about life, about spirituality, and ultimately about who we are. The deepest spiritual truths are not just intellectual abstractions; they are a living, breathing Presence at the heart of all life. I invite you to use this book as a springboard to ever deeper inquiry into this Presence, which is who you really are.

Note: This book is a collection of my articles, transcriptions of talks from satsangs (spiritual meetings), and posts from my blog. Although the book is arranged into sections, you are free to wander through the essays as you please.

At the end of each part is a link to a webpage where you can listen to an mp3 recording of a talk given in satsang. These mp3s are only available to purchasers of this book and are offered to expand on the material in each section.

CHAPTER 1

AWARENESS

Awareness is a fundamental quality of our Being. Awareness is always here in everything and in every experience. We need to be aware in order to experience. If you could turn off your awareness, then the world, your body, your thoughts, and everything else would simply disappear. Since we are constantly having experiences, it must be true that awareness is always here.

And yet, what a mystery this awareness is. Why is it we have this capacity to register and notice what happens? Where does this capacity come from? Does it come from our brain and nervous system or from something beyond our physical form? Are you aware of anything at all in this moment? What is that awareness like? How do you know you are aware right now? And what if the source of awareness is also the source of everything else?

Because spiritual seekers seek expanded awareness, they often overlook the mystery of the awareness that is already here. Just as a single drop of water is wet, the awareness that is reading these words has all of the qualities of your true nature as pure awareness. Does the part of you that is already awake need to wake up, or is it already profoundly and mysteriously aware? Just for a moment, instead of seeking more awareness, find out more about the awareness that is already here.

The awareness that is here in this moment is alive, spacious, discriminating, and full of love. Everything that really matters is found in this awareness. Love, peace, and joy flow from within us to the experiences we have of the world. Seeking the source of peace or love in the world is like looking for the source of the water in the puddle that forms under a water faucet. Not only is the source here within us, but it is flowing right now as the simple awareness that is reading these words.

Awareness Is Never the Same Way Twice

Q: *How can I become aware?*

A: You can't become something you already are. I invite you to explore the awareness that is already here. What is it that is reading these words? Are you aware right now of the words on this page? What is that awareness like? Where does awareness come from in this very moment?

Everything that really matters, including peace, joy, and fulfillment, is found in this ever-present, simple awareness. We tend to overlook awareness because it is so ordinary, and yet awareness is actually a profound mystery. Many mistakenly think that awareness is something they need to seek or become. Awareness is something we can explore and recognize more fully, but to do that, no seeking or becoming is required. In fact, seeking gets in the way because when we are seeking, we tend to overlook the experience of awareness that is already here.

Awareness is not an object, and it doesn't come from an object: Awareness is a capacity of empty space or alive Presence, which is not a thing or a person. So when you explore awareness, you can become "spacey" or disoriented. It is normal to feel spacey when you are exploring space! We aren't used to directing our attention to emptiness, or the nothingness behind our eyes. So we may look away and go looking for something else instead. But what happens right now if you simply pay attention to the space behind your eyes? What happens if you pay attention to the empty silence your thoughts are appearing in? What happens if you pay attention to your aliveness?

There is no right or wrong experience of awareness. There are many different flavors, or qualities, of awareness, or aliveness. You have always been experiencing some quality of your true nature. Since awareness is what experiences every experience, you have been exploring your capacity for awareness all along, in every experience you have ever had. And yet, there is always more to discover about this capacity to be aware.

The one thing you can be sure of is that your experience of awareness will never be the same way twice. The nature of Presence, or Being, is that it never has the same experience twice. So you will never be done exploring the limitless capacities of your nature as awareness, even though you don't need to go anywhere or seek anything to find it. Awareness is always showing you a new face, a new disguise, a new possibility. The only question is: Will you acknowledge and savor the unique flavor that awareness has right now?

We Are All Baby Ducks

The following is from the book Living from the Heart *by Nirmala, available here: http://endless-satsang.com/free*

Realizing your true nature as awareness would be incredibly simple except for one thing: This awareness that you are can be shaped. Just like water takes on the shape of the container you pour it into, this awareness that you are is shaped by your thoughts, feelings, desires, hopes, dreams, worries, sensations, and experiences. It is shaped by everything that happens. Sometimes this shaping is so strong that it seems the awareness has gotten very small and that you have gotten very small. This is not really a problem, as the awareness itself is not harmed, and it can always expand again.

This awareness is not only temporarily shaped by experience, but can become imprinted onto an experience or an object in awareness. You may have heard of how baby ducks become imprinted in the first few hours of their lives: They will follow whatever or whomever they are first aware of, usually the mother duck. However, they can also be imprinted on anything, including a scientist who is studying them, in which case, they will follow the scientist around.

There is nothing wrong with this; following their mother wherever she goes helps baby ducks survive in the wild. It is an inherent capacity of all awareness to become imprinted, or conditioned, in this way. Every time an experience leaves a lasting impression in your awareness, you have been imprinted, or conditioned, by that experience.

However for humans, this imprinting is more complicated than for ducks. You can be imprinted onto many different things. One of the things you are most imprinted on is your body. You are so strongly imprinted onto your body that most of the time your awareness follows your body wherever it goes—just like a baby duck follows its mother. Check it out: Get up and walk into another room. Does your awareness stay in the room you just left or follow your body into the other room? We are all baby ducks when it comes to our bodies.

Another thing you are profoundly imprinted on is your own mind or thoughts (from here on when thoughts are mentioned, it will refer to the entire range of internal experience: thoughts, beliefs, feelings, desires, hopes, fantasies, etc.). So when a thought, a fear, or a longing arises, your awareness flows to that. Check it out: When you stop thinking one thought and begin thinking another, does your awareness stay on the original thought, or does it follow your thoughts wherever they go? Isn't it kind of like a baby duck following its momma across the pond and out into the meadow and then into the creek?

You have been imprinted onto your physical body and your mind. This isn't bad. Just as with baby ducks, it does have some benefits for your survival, although not always: Just as a baby duck will follow its mother onto a busy freeway, your awareness will follow your thoughts into all kinds of silly and sometimes dangerous places.

Since you are almost always aware of your body and your mind (because awareness follows your body and mind around), you come to the mistaken conclusion that you are your body and your mind. You fail to recognize that what you are is the empty, spacious awareness that the body and mind appear in. You assume, since they are almost always here, "I am the body and the mind."

This is a simple and completely understandable mistake. Unfortunately, it is also a colossal mistake and the source of all your suffering. It's as if you had a fly on your nose that stuck around so long that you decided you were the fly. Imagine how confused you would feel and act if you believed you were a fly! You would spend all day eating rotten food and trying to mate with other flies!

Sensing Awareness

I invite you to take a moment to just sense the awareness in this room. Just sense the awareness right where you are sitting and the awareness all around. Very simply, awareness is a kind of brightness that lights things up, that notices things. This is simple awareness. Awareness doesn't stop when you or I stop talking or doing something. No matter what is going on, awareness is here noticing whatever is happening. It might be scanning around, noticing this thought and then that thought, noticing this sensation and then another. Just notice the simple ordinary awareness that's here right now.

Everything you've ever sought, wanted, or desired—all the peace, joy, satisfaction, fulfillment, and richness of existence you've looked for your whole life—is here right now in the flow of awareness. If you were going to hide these things, awareness is a really good place to hide them because it's the last place anybody would think to look. We never think to look in our ordinary experience, and yet peace, joy, and love are all here in awareness, either in expression or in potential. This limitless reservoir of love, of Presence, of joy, of satisfaction is always right here whether you're tapping into it or not, whether you're noticing it or not. It's just here.

This simple awareness also has a capacity to be shaped. It can be directed. So if I say something about elephants, your awareness starts flowing to ideas about elephants. Or if I point to the ceiling beams, your awareness goes there. All we have to do is think about something, and awareness flows to that.

Awareness has the capacity to be shaped by anything you or I say. In fact, everything that happens shapes your awareness. If there's a sudden loud noise, that noise will shape your awareness. If someone talks to you, that will shape your awareness. Everything that's happening right now in the room, every subtle movement, every chemical reaction happening in your body as a result of what you ate recently is all shaping your awareness. On even subtler levels, the feeling state of others nearby is affecting you right now. It's shaping your awareness and having an impact on you.

This is natural. Part of the potential of this awareness is that it has an incredible capacity to take on shape. That's how creation happens: Awareness, or Presence, gets shaped into form. This includes subtler forms of shaping, like thought.

This shaped awareness doesn't feel limitless—on the contrary. For example, when awareness is shaped by a physical pain, it gets very narrow, especially when you're lying in bed and the lights are off and nothing else is happening. It's amazing how a stubbed toe can suddenly fill your entire awareness. So when awareness is shaped, it doesn't seem so limitless because it has a shape—it has a form, a container. An experience, a thought, or sensations add a limited quality to the experience of awareness.

In gatherings like satsang, we do something unusual. We talk about the awareness itself. What's the nature of it? What's it like? And yet, awareness isn't something you can really be aware of. You can't really be aware of awareness because awareness is not a thing. The best you can ever do is to catch a sense of it, to sense some of its qualities, or at least be curious about it. You can't fully catch awareness in awareness.

Yet, anytime I mention awareness, that shapes awareness, and everybody starts looking for it. Where is awareness? Is it under the chair? Is it behind the door? Awareness goes off looking for awareness, and so awareness is shaped by this concept of awareness. Once awareness takes on any shape, even the shape of the concept of awareness, it becomes smaller. Anytime awareness takes on a shape, awareness is naturally smaller than its total potential.

Even then, everything that really matters, everything that really satisfies and fulfills us is already right here and now in this awareness, no matter how awareness is being shaped, no matter how small awareness has become. That's the startling thing. Everything that matters is here even when awareness is being shaped.

Everything shapes our awareness, but words and concepts are the primary ways humans shape consciousness. For spiritual seekers, ideas about enlightenment shape their consciousness, including the possible idea that enlightenment means the end of the shaping of awareness. Because our awareness is constantly being shifted and shaped by everything that happens, the range of experience that is possible shows us how flexible awareness is. Awareness is shaped, but the shape is temporary, and so the awareness itself is not harmed. The recognition that awareness cannot be harmed is even more valuable than a profound but temporary spiritual experience.

This recognition allows the deeper realization that it doesn't really matter what shape your awareness has. In fact, if you could be in an expanded state of consciousness all the time, you would never discover that it doesn't matter what shape your awareness has, because your awareness would never have a shape. Without any shape to awareness, awareness is totally silent, totally still. If you were to stay in an expanded state of consciousness, there would be no way to find out about awareness. What good does all that awareness do you if you never use it to dip your toe into the full range of experience?

The important question is: What is awareness like right now? That's where you'll discover this limitless abundance. That's the gift that's being pointed to right now—it is the opportunity to discover the truth of your awareness just as it is right now, because when you find out that awareness is complete just the way it is, then it doesn't matter anymore how it's being shaped. It doesn't matter what thought is arising right now or if no thought is arising right now. Those are just the particulars of how the awareness is being temporarily shaped. It's natural that your awareness is being shaped right now because it is always being shaped.

The opportunity is to find out that it doesn't matter how awareness is being shaped. Find out if there is really anything wrong right now with awareness? Does it really matter if it's chasing after something or confused or happy or sad or sleepy or awake? Does that stuff matter when you have a limitless supply of awareness itself? Especially when all of the love, peace, and joy you have ever wanted are already present in the awareness that is here right now.

Becoming More Aware of Your Ribs

Q: Are spiritual practices necessary, or are they a hindrance, consolidating the sense of an individual self? In particular, my mind creates the seeming problem of what to do and busies itself with this, even as I try to observe it. Do I spend short moments each day resting as awareness, or do I inquire into myself? Or do I try to combine these? And when I spend time inquiring into myself, I find thoughts swim in: "What question should I ask myself? Should I ask more than one question? Is 'Who am I?' the question to ask or 'Where am I?' or 'From where does the I thought arise?' How often during the day should I ask these questions?" and so on.

I think in part my mind's busyness stems from having read a lot of different nondual texts, all of which recommend different approaches, and I find that all of them speak to me. Sometimes I want to watch the breath or attend to the inner body, sometimes I want to observe thought, and sometimes I want to inquire into the "I." But then I become aware than I'm hopping from channel to channel, as if I'm trying to find the right practice—which I know doesn't exist.

A: My suggestion is to try all of the approaches and all of the questions and be really curious about what you experience with each and every moment of practice or non-practice. This consciousness that you are is affected by everything—that is why we call it consciousness! And so every form of inquiry question will have a different effect on you. In addition, every time you ask the same question, the experience will be different, since your consciousness is being affected by a wide range of influences in each unique moment.

So how is it different to ask, "Who am I?" versus, "Where does the 'I' thought come from?" You can also play with an even simpler form of the question: "Am I?" What is the effect of hopping from channel to channel with a wide range of questions and practices? And what is it like to simply sit with one question or practice for a while longer? And what is it like in between the questions and in between the thoughts? What effect on your consciousness does silence have?

This underlying curiosity is the heart of the practices. The point of practice is not to get somewhere, but to show you something about yourself as you already are. Curiosity is not something you can get better at—you already are very curious, as is clear from all the questions you asked. Spiritual practice isn't meant to make you better at the practice or to answer your questions. It's meant to put you in touch with what is already true about your awareness. It's kind of like practicing having ribs: You can't get any better at having a ribcage, but you can become more aware of the ribs you already have.

With this simple result in mind, there is no right or wrong way to practice. It also doesn't matter if you practice or not; this innate curiosity of your awareness will still be here. Often when we hear that it doesn't matter if we practice or not, we assume that means there is no reason to practice. But it is also true that there is no reason *not* to practice. And often the most authentic and natural expression of this curiosity is through some kind of inquiry or practice. So when you do practice, enjoy it!

Spiritual practice doesn't cause you to be curious or more aware. But the reason why the impulse for spiritual practice naturally occurs when this curiosity starts to dive deeply into awareness is that spiritual practices are about awareness. So just as directing awareness to your ribs doesn't cause you to have ribs but it does make it more likely you will be aware of your ribs, so directing your curiosity toward awareness doesn't cause you to be more aware, but it can make it more likely you will notice the awareness that is already here.

Curiosity is just one of many qualities that awareness has. Awareness is also loving, compassionate, peaceful, strong, powerful, and wise. So in playing with curiosity and awareness, you never know what you will discover next.

Life as a Sitcom

Life is like a sitcom. If you think about it, almost every sitcom has one plot, although there are many versions of it. Basically, the plot is that at the beginning of the show someone says or does something foolish. Someone tells a white lie, makes a mistake, or doesn't tell somebody something that they should have. That's the setup.

On *I Love Lucy*, Lucy loses her wedding ring. Or on *Seinfeld*, George tells his date that he's a member of Mensa to impress her. Someone makes a little mistake or tells a little white lie or causes some misunderstanding. Then most of the half hour is taken up with the main character trying to cover up, hide, or make up for this mistake. He or she has to sort of fake it to keep everybody fooled. Then, of course, the situation gets more and more ridiculous as the story progresses, and eventually the pretense can no longer be kept up. The character has told too many lies, has too many balls in the air, and can't keep it up, so the truth comes out. Finally, Ricky turns to Lucy and says, "Lucy, tell me what's really going on." And Lucy starts to cry and admits that she lost her wedding ring, and then all is forgiven and life goes on.

We live this plot in a lot of ways. It's the form that a lot of the drama in our life takes on. You might even say our human life is like a sitcom because we make one really simple mistake at the beginning: We assume that we are the body, the mind, and the personality that is generated by that misidentification.

Then, because it's not real, because it's not true, we spend our whole life trying to cover up how incomplete, unreal, fake, and untrue it feels to believe that we are this body-mind. We go through all kinds of crazy machinations just to keep the illusion going, to keep the little white lie going—until the lie starts to wear itself out. Eventually, you can't keep yourself fooled.

Like in the sitcom, awareness of the truth eventually becomes too strong for the cover-up to continue. So awareness of the truth is the antidote to all of our struggles, all of the effort we go through to try to keep our illusions going. The antidote to the lie is simply awareness. When awareness and our misunderstandings come together, when we become aware of our mistake, our false beliefs and identities can't withstand that light and attention, and they start to dissolve.

There's no formula for how fast that dissolving happens. The dissolving of our misunderstandings and illusions isn't something we do; it's not a further activity of our mind. It happens simply by bringing awareness to our mind. Dissolving happens whenever we become aware of what is actually present and true, beyond our mistaken conclusions. So a lot of spiritual teachings and practices direct us toward bringing awareness to our experience and slowing down and noticing what is actually happening.

To bring our awareness to our mind, it helps to slow down, because our mind is moving so fast that awareness can barely keep up. When our mind is going a mile a minute, when our lives are going a mile a minute, there's little opportunity for this dissolving to have the time and space to happen. So that is why spiritual practices are designed to slow us down. They bring us to a pause in our experience. The most obvious one is meditation, just sitting. Whether you use a meditative technique or you just sit, meditation slows things down quite a bit. It allows awareness to touch what's happening right now.

Of course, often the first thing awareness touches is all that activity of the mind. Spiritual practices bring awareness to the present moment in a way that not only touches the present moment, but caresses and really tastes the moment. When we slow down, awareness can really take in what's happening right now. And if what is happening is a busy mind, then we experience how busy our mind is.

The invitation is to slow down, to touch your present moment experience with awareness, whether what you're experiencing is a thought, a feeling, sensations, a yearning, a sense of lack or emptiness, or the overall busyness of your mind. The invitation is to slow down and actually experience what is happening now—shine some of this light that we call awareness on what's happening right now. The invitation is to take a moment with the busyness of your mind or with your emotions or with that yearning or with a sensation you are having.

The particular content of our experience is not the most important thing. Our tendency is to focus on the content of our experience and to evaluate that: "Is it working? Am I getting there? Is this spiritual? Is this getting me something?" And yet doing this is what keeps us going faster and faster. Slowing down means giving awareness to whatever *experience* you are having right now.

What really matters is the awareness itself. What really matters is our strange capacity to register bodily sensations, experience thought, hear the voices in our head, and know what we're feeling. How do we do that? What happens when awareness fully touches the thought, feeling, or sensation? What really matters right now is the awareness that's taking in these words and noticing your thoughts. This awareness might also be noticing a feeling. Or it might be noticing one or more sensations—something about the chair you're sitting on, the air temperature, or just the sounds in the room.

What happens right now if you just slow down and experience whatever is happening right now? If it's a thought, what happens if you slow down and really experience not so much the content of that thought, but the arising of thought, the strangeness of thought? What happens if you slow down and notice if there is an emotion or the absence of emotional energy? What happens if you stay with the emotion of this moment or stay with the absence of an emotion?

You can do this in the same way you would eat chocolate. Ideally, when you're eating chocolate, you put it in your mouth and see how long you can hold out before you have to swallow. You want to let the taste buds touch every molecule of chocolate as it melts in your mouth. What happens right now if you touch your thoughts in the same way—if you look with that same delicacy at the arising patterns of your thoughts and take some time to be with them just as they are?

A lot is made of the moments in life when things dissolve dramatically, like when you have a profound spiritual experience. But you can also develop an appreciation for everyday awareness, even when the dissolving is more like a creek carving a canyon. Releasing some of our structures or stuck places can take a long time. Uncovering the truth is rich, not just when there is a big breakthrough, but right from the beginning—once you're willing to be with your awareness.

All the richness that comes in big waves in a moment of breakthrough is actually always present. It is always available. What's satisfying is the awareness—even when it comes to chocolate. Chocolate is most satisfying when we slow down and fully experience it. It's why all the things we take the greatest pleasure in are satisfying—because when something pleasurable is happening, we naturally tend to slow down. In that slowing down, we experience more of this pure, rich flow of awareness that is in and of itself pleasurable.

Fears Are True, but Fortunately Not Very True

Q: Recent world events have brought up a lot of fear and frustration for me. It is difficult to deal with the emotions that come up around all of the disaster on the world stage. Accepting these events placidly seems impossible. Can I ask how you are coping and how you would advise handling the fear and sadness that the world situation brings up?

A: The problem with our fears is that they are all potentially true. Anything we can imagine could happen, so our fears have some truth to them. However, none of our fears have much truth, and most of our fears have a ridiculously small amount of truth to them.

First of all, none of our fears have come true yet. If they had, we wouldn't be fearing them anymore! So in that sense, all fear only exists as thoughts in our minds. Fear only exists as the movement of thought and feeling, and that is a very small existence. Yet, we have been taught to focus on our thoughts and feelings. We have been asked repeatedly, "What do you think?" and "What do you feel?" As a result, we pay close attention to the movement of thoughts and emotions in our mind and body: "What do I think about this?" "How do I feel about that?" So even though their actual existence is very slight, thoughts and feelings can seem much more important and true than they really are. We even use the argument, "Well, that's what I think!" to make a point, as if the mere fact that we think something makes it true!

Secondly, even when something we were afraid of happens, it never happens exactly as we imagined. Regarding many of the stories in the news right now, if a worst case scenario were to happen, it is still unlikely that all of the disastrous consequences predicted would actually come true. And who knows, any particularly dramatic episode might actually shift our world into a new and more productive direction. So the specific content of our fears is never a very complete picture of what will or can happen.

Even though our fears are not very accurate or important, they still can contract our awareness. It is this contraction of awareness that allows us to become hypnotized by the media and its fear-producing stories. The contraction of awareness is a kind of hypnosis or trance that fear triggers in us.

With any form of hypnosis, the antidote is awareness. The more aware you become of the experiential quality of your thoughts and fears—how they contract you—the less hypnotized you will be by the content of your thoughts and fears. Thought mostly functions to contract our awareness and put us into various trance states. This is not a mistake, but the contraction this causes gets old after a while. Then we naturally feel drawn to experiencing the flow of awareness without any trance-like illusions getting in the way.

Years ago, I studied a form of therapeutic hypnosis. The instructor explained that by understanding more about how hypnotic trances are triggered, we would become less susceptible to them. We would recognize that someone or something was hypnotizing us and then we could choose to follow the hypnotic suggestion or not.

One method for inducing trance is to get someone to focus their awareness. The classic example is getting someone to focus on a swinging object, like a pocket watch. Similarly, the dramatic and extreme images of dire possible future outcomes get us to focus intently on the images on the television. We become hypnotized by these images. Television uses many of the hypnotic techniques I learned. Even more amazing is how our own mind uses those same techniques to shape our own awareness. We have learned what images and thoughts trigger a trance in us, and so we become hypnotized by our own thoughts! This is not a mistake, as consciousness wants to experience every possible state, including the trance state we call fear.

However, at any moment, you can wake up from your fear-induced trances. Notice the contraction of awareness that comes with every fear. This contraction is a sign that your awareness is leaving something out. The more contracted your awareness is, the more expanded your unawareness is! You can wake up from a fear-induced trance by simply noticing what else is true besides the content of your fearful thoughts or by becoming very curious about the feelings and sensations in your body: How true is the content of that thought? What else is true? What else is possible? How do you even know what you are thinking right now? How do you know you are afraid? What sensations are present that let you know you are afraid? Are they actually bad sensations or just different sensations?

Directing your awareness in this way to the mental structures and visceral sensations of the fear can dissolve the fear. Like the highway mirages that disappear as soon as we get closer to them, as you get closer to and more curious about your fears, they tend to disappear. All that has disappeared is a thought or feeling that was shaping your awareness. Without that thought or feeling, your awareness expands again to include more of the truth. It turns out that the biggest truths are the truths of love, divine intelligence, and the mystery and beauty of life. These bigger truths are not very scary at all! At any moment, you can turn away from the television screen or from the "television screen" of your own mind and see what else is here besides your thoughts and fears.

Personally, I am fascinated by all of this. I occasionally enjoy watching or reading the news and observing the reactions the news can trigger in me and in others. I also enjoy the moments when awareness penetrates into all of this in a new way. For example, as you become more curious about your own fear, you may notice how much of our society is driven by fear. Most political battles are between one set of fears and another set of fears. Neither side can see how their fears limit their view, and a narrow view naturally leads to extreme or imbalanced approaches. The antidote is always more awareness and truth. The truth really does set you free.

Is There One or Many? Yes!

Q: *I'm reading your book* Living from the Heart *for the second time and still don't understand something about aware space. I understand that who I really am is aware space and not my body, mind, and personality. But when there is another person here, they most likely know me as a body, mind, and personality. When I'm with another person, I'm also relating to their body, mind, and personality because that is in my awareness. This seems contradictory. Can you explain this further?*

A: Your question boils down to the question: "Is there one awareness or many?" The answer is yes! There is one awareness acting and appearing as many. The mind doesn't understand when two apparently opposite things are both true, but it turns out that oneness and multiplicity aren't really opposites. They are different qualities, or expressions, of one thing. The simplest example is your own hand. It has many fingers, and yet, your hand is also one thing. The many fingers are one expression, or aspect, of your hand, but the oneness of the hand as a whole is another quality of the same thing.

We are able to experience both the obvious uniqueness of our individual perspective, as you described, and the deeper truth of oneness. But like all deeper truths, the experience of oneness is more subtle and therefore more challenging to experience, although it is also more universal and ever-present. Since oneness is here in every moment, we tend to overlook it, just as we don't generally notice the air we breathe because we are so used to it and take it for granted.

The fact that you can experience your own and other people's body, mind, and personality, doesn't need to contradict the sense that you are aware space. The source of awareness is infinite in its potential. It creates everything that exists, and one thing it seems to love to create is the experience of individuality. I invite you to read the fairytale at the end of *Beyond No Self* (included as Appendix 1 in this book) which is a fanciful story about how oneness manages to appear as many. It offers a perspective that suggests that every apparent individual is also infinite in potential. That is the great thing about infinity: Every *part* of infinity can also be infinite!

Be Curious About What Is

I invite you to be curious about whatever is happening right now. I invite you to rest from doing anything. But rest with your eyes open and give your full awareness to what is already here. The invitation is to rest with curiosity.

But, of course, both resting and curiosity can be used to avoid experience instead—you can avoid things by resting. You can even rest your way right out of awareness by going to sleep. You can also get so curious about how things *should* be and what *could* happen—about your ideas, beliefs, and fantasies—that your curiosity takes you right out of your present moment experience. How clever of us to have discovered how to leave the present moment!

It's possible, instead, to simply be curious about the way things already are. The art of resting and curiosity is learning to apply them to the present moment. To the mind, focusing on what's already here can seem like a waste of time. But you can give your devotion, your focus, your curiosity, and your allowing acceptance to what's already present right now. The place where curiosity and resting come alive is in the experience you are having right now. There's no seeking required, no searching, no movement, or journey to something else that's necessary first. Seeking is a good way to delay being curious, delay resting, when you can just rest and be curious right now, just rest with and be curious about the sensations that are present right in this moment.

There isn't anything wrong with being curious about something other than your present moment experience, but also find out what happens if you spend your awareness on your experience just the way it is, on what's happening right now.

The Qualities of Awareness: A Talk by Nirmala

An mp3 recording of a talk given in satsang is available to purchasers of this book at:

http://endless-satsang.com/part1mp3

Chapter 2

SPACE

Space is another fundamental quality of our Being and of all existence. Without space, everything would disappear. Without space, where would you put everything? What a miracle it is that we have space for everything! Where does all of this space come from? Why is there a here and a there and an infinite number of other places all made up of the empty dimension we call space?

Surprisingly, although space is empty, it is also alive and aware. We usually think of space as nothing, as empty and dry. But this nothing, or no-thing, is the source of everything. Space is the source of the awareness that is reading these words and of the love, peace, and joy that come with awareness. Space has an infinite energy and capacity within it, which creates and becomes all the forms, bodies, and expressions of this universe.

However, we tend to see the emptiness of space as a problem, as something to be filled, as an experience of lack or incompleteness. We are taught at a very young age that any emptiness we feel is filled from outside: Our hunger and thirst are provided for by others. Our physical emptiness and discomfort are relieved by our mother or other caretaker. Even before we have language, we've developed a conditioned response to inner sensations of emptiness or lack. We have learned to look outside ourselves to satisfy any sense of emptiness or lack. This aspect of our conditioning takes us away from the true source of our soul's nourishment and love, which is in the space itself.

As a result of this conditioning, we develop very little familiarity with the experience of space itself because space is felt to be a problematic emptiness or lack. We are too busy trying to resolve or reduce the sensations of emptiness or lack to explore space itself in greater depth: What is the sensation of emptiness like? How does nothingness feel when it appears inside us? How big is the empty space? Can the emptiness inside actually feel bigger than our body? How is that possible? And what is the texture or quality of the space that seems to be lacking something? Is it completely clear and lacking all qualities, or is the emptiness dark or bright, heavy or light, dry or moist? If the open space inside us feels lacking in something we want, like love or a sense of our own worth, is there anything else that is present in the space? And finally, does the emptiness hurt us or cause us any harm? Or is it our resistance to the feelings of lack and our effort to change our experience that cause us to suffer?

Questions like these can inspire curiosity about the emptiness itself. We might even discover that emptiness is a freeing experience and not necessarily a problem. Empty space is the softest thing in the universe, and it is very low maintenance. There's nothing it can do to harm you, and there's nothing you can do to harm it. Perhaps the most surprising discovery of all is that empty space is the true source of everything that really matters in life. All of the peace, joy, and love we experience come directly from the still, silent, pure emptiness of our true nature. It turns out the biggest problem in our life, our sense of lack or incompleteness, is actually our greatest blessing. What a surprise to find so much richness coming from such an unpromising source.

The biggest surprise of all is when we discover that space is what we really are. We are the alive, infinite potential of aware space that is experiencing the body, the room, and this beautiful world of mystery and love. It is space itself that is aware of everything we experience. This aware space is soft and gentle, empty and full, infinite and unharmable, and the source of everything that matters. What a delightful shock to discover that this mysterious space is what we really are!

What Is Found in Lack?

Q: How do I go about exploring the sense of lack? Here's my attempt: From the perspective of feeling, the sense of lack is a tension and sense of anxiety. The tension can be felt to different degrees everywhere in the body. The anxiety seems to be in the lower belly, the stomach, and the chest. The thoughts that go along with it are: "People know something I don't. I have to get more information, more knowledge. Something is missing. Maybe I can get what I need from a teacher or book. I'm not enough. I need something more. I have to prove myself. I have to work hard and earn enlightenment. Something in the future could bring me what I want. The future could also bring disaster. I'm so vulnerable. I'm incomplete, insecure, and lacking in confidence." That seems to be its voice at the moment. I still feel like I'm missing something in my exploration of missing something! How do you suggest I meet this sense of something missing? What can I do?

A: That's a wonderful start to your exploration. You can also become curious about the actual "hole" or emptiness in the center of the feeling of lack. Directing your attention to this sensation of lack will bring to awareness all the voices, memories, and conditioning associated with the experience of lack, which need to be seen and allowed to be there. Just allow any associations to arise and be seen and continue to direct your awareness to the emptiness or sense of lack.

If you stay with this process long enough, often a deeper layer of conditioning will come to the surface, which may appear as feelings, such as sadness, anger, or fear. Or you might experience a deeper layer of your true nature, which may appear as a quality of essence, or Being, such as love, peace, or joy. Surprisingly, what often arises in the lack is the very thing you felt you were lacking. For instance, love can be found in the place where you experience a lack of love, and worth can be found in a place where you experience a lack of self-worth. There's no formula for this exploration, as whenever you look within, the experience unfolds differently. But all you really need to do is trust and explore whatever shows up.

Even the deeper experiences of essence are empty at their core. When you touch this emptiness, the invitation is to go even deeper into the emptiness. Infinite layers of essential aspects of your Being are then discovered to be hiding another deeper layer of emptiness. Surprisingly, the doorway to the deeper reality is often the place where it seems emptiest.

Self-Inquiry

The following is from the book Nothing Personal *by Nirmala, which is available at http://endless-satsang.com/free*

Beyond focusing on the content of our experience and even beyond noticing whether we're expanded or contracted, a wonderful question is: "Who or what is experiencing this?" This is a variation of the classic self-inquiry question, "Who am I?"

As I was going through my email the other day, I ran across a quote from A *Course in Miracles* that essentially said you'll never find satisfaction in the world. This assertion is at the core of most spiritual teachings. Spiritual teachings and practices attempt to turn us in another direction, away from the usual places we look for satisfaction. They're designed to shift our focus from the world of form to Beingness. Self-inquiry is one technique for doing that. In self-inquiry, we simply ask, "Who am I?" or "What am I?" or a variation on that: "Who is having this experience?" When you look to see who is having this experience, you don't find anyone. There's nothing there. The experiencer can't be experienced, just as the eye can't see itself. You don't find any *thing*, nothing you can touch or see or hear.

When *nothing* is discovered, people often keep looking for *something* they think they're supposed to find. It's only natural to look somewhere else when you don't find anything. We don't expect that *nothing* is the answer. So we go back to our mind for the answer—we think about it, check in our memory, or imagine a good answer—instead of just staying with the question. But inquiry done only with the mind is dry—it lacks juice. After a while, because this experience is not very rich, the mind often gets bored and quits. There isn't much in it for the mind.

Another way to ask the question is with your whole Heart. You ask it with everything you've got, as if your life depended on it. If you ask the question with this kind of passion and intensity, it will bring you beyond what the mind is able to figure out. When you ask it with your whole Heart and you don't find an answer, you just stay there, not knowing. You just let yourself not know. There's nothing but that space, and you just stay present to that space, to that sense of there being nothing behind your eyes, nothing behind your thoughts, nothing behind your feelings. Instead of turning back to thing-ness when you don't find anything, you just stay there in the no-thing-ness and get curious about it. Nothing—what's that like?

In looking and finding nothing, what you discover is even more space. Staying with the question "Who am I?" opens up space. Nothingness is very spacious; there's a lot of room in it. When you stay in that nothingness, you discover that there's a lot of stuff in that space, stuff that is real in a way that the stuff in the world has never been real. What moves in that space are true qualities of Being, such as love, compassion, insight, and strength.

Every time you turn toward Beingness, a different quality shows up. Being has an infinite number of qualities, which show up fresh and different in every moment. These qualities can seem to exist in another dimension, as they have a depth and solidity about them that is more real than physical objects.

These qualities have been there in the nothingness all along, and as you stay with the nothingness, they begin to be apparent. One way of staying with the inward focus is by repeatedly asking the question, "Who Am I?" Stay with the question even when you experience nothing and have no idea who you are. Just ask, "Who or what doesn't know?"

Become a Lake

Someone shared this wonderful story with me on Facebook (the original author is unknown):

An aging Hindu master grew tired of his apprentice complaining, so one morning the master sent his apprentice for some salt. When the apprentice returned, the master instructed the unhappy young man to put a handful of salt in a glass of water and then drink it.

"How does it taste?" the master asked.

"Bitter," spit the apprentice.

The master chuckled and then asked the young man to take the same amount of salt and put it in the lake. The two walked in silence to a nearby lake, and once the apprentice swirled his handful of salt in the water, the old man said, "Now drink from the lake."

As the water dripped down the young man's chin, the master asked, "How does it taste?"

"Much fresher," remarked the apprentice.

"Do you taste the salt?" asked the master.

"No," said the young man.

At this, the master sat beside the young man who so reminded him of himself and took his hands, offering, "The pain of life is pure salt, no more, no less. The amount of pain in life remains the same, exactly the same. But the amount of bitterness we taste depends on the container we put the pain in. So when you are in pain, the only thing you can do is to enlarge your sense of things... Stop being a glass. Become a lake."

Giving Space to Everything

Q: There's a person I have to deal with who keeps pushing my buttons. She says awful things to me. She did that recently, and I have a hard time dealing with how angry I feel. I'd like to tell her that I never want to see her again, but I'm taking care of her cats, and I have to see her again. I feel like there's something wrong with me or I'm deficient because I can't just tell her where to go—the anger is directed at myself. I love taking care of those cats, and because of this, I bite my tongue and just let her words go in one ear and out the other. But there's still this part of me that feels like not standing up to her diminishes me.

A: So what's it like right now as you describe this? What's the sense of not standing up to her like, how does the self-diminishing feel?

Q: It's hard to get into it because I have a headache. I've had a headache all day.

A: What happens if you give that headache a lot of space? What if you just let the headache be as big as it is? Give it lots of room to be here just the way it is.

Q: That has never even entered my mind.

A: This is an invitation to give away your awareness by letting things have space. There's so much awareness here that you can waste it. And what better thing to waste awareness on than a headache, right? The headache doesn't even have anything to do with your issue. So we're really getting into the wasting of awareness. What happens if you just give your headache lots and lots of space to be the way it is, the size it is?

Q: *Well, there's a certain quietness about it that I like.*

A: It turns out there's lots and lots of room here, including room for the sensations you call a headache.

Q: *But I didn't come up to talk about that.*

A: So let's just play a bit. That's all we're here for is to play. You found out there's room for the headache. What happens now if you give space to the thought that there's something wrong with you, that somehow you are deficient? What happens if you give space to that thought and to the whole bundle of thoughts about what is wrong with you. What happens if you give the whole bundle lots and lots of space?

Q: *You mean just allow those thoughts to be?*

A: Just allow them—find out what happens if you waste your spacious awareness on them.

Q: *It's kind of fun if you just let them be here.*

A: There's no suffering in that.

Q: *There's no fight in that. I'm used to fighting.*

A: So? There's also space to fight in. We're not taking anything away; we're giving everything space to be. There probably is some real anger under all that self-doubt.

Q: *There certainly was earlier.*

A: So you can give space to that. Why leave anger out?

Q: *Well, you're not supposed to be angry.*

A: So give space to the belief that you're not supposed to be angry. It's a totally natural thing to believe because you were probably told that many times. You were taught that it's not okay to be angry. So it's very natural that some resistance to anger appears, but what happens if you give your resistance to being angry lots of space to be here?

Q: *Then I calm down.*

A: Giving lots of space to things can be like filling a tea cup with a fire hose. When you try to fill a teacup with a fire hose, water gets in a lot of other places than just the teacup! So when you start giving space and allowing your awareness to just flow to what's here, a lot more is allowed than just the original belief. You'll discover that there's not only room for that belief, but also for a lot of other things.

Q: *So it's kind of one big OK?*

A: Yes, that is the nature of awareness—because it can't be harmed, right?

Q: *Awareness can't be harmed?*

A: It's empty. How can you harm empty space? We're just playing here right? So when you're playing you might as well go for it, right?

Q: *We're playing with Monopoly money?*

A: Exactly! It's like having a limitless supply of free Monopoly money, a limitless supply of awareness. So what happens right now if you give space to this person, just the way she is?

Q: *Whenever that happens, it feels good.*

A: That's because another word for this flow of aware space is love. So anytime you're giving it away, guess what? You're immersing yourself in love. Notice what happens if you keep giving space to this person, including all of her behaviors. You can give her space equal in size to the entire state of Texas if you need to. You can give her lots and lots of space. At the same time you are giving her space, you can also give yourself lots of space.

Q: *It always makes me feel better when I just allow her to be herself. But when I can't do that and she really bothers me, then I feel I should do something about that.*

A: That's why you also need to give as much space to yourself, to all the feelings that arise and to all the reactions you have to her behavior. Give yourself lots of space, even if that sometimes means literally getting up and giving yourself a lot of space from this other person. Space is limitless. So remember, you can give space to everything, not just to her and to yourself, but to everyone and everything. Also you can give space to all the feelings you have about her and about everything: all the judgments, all the resistance, and all the feelings you have about her cats, your anger, speaking up, and your headache. Just include, include, include,

include. Find out for yourself; don't take my word for anything. Find out for yourself if you can run out of space or awareness.

Pointers for Giving Space

Here are some pointers for giving space that are also found in Living from the Heart *(to sample or purchase the book, go to http://endless-satsang.com/free):*

Another way to move into a more spacious perspective is to simply give space to your experience. You can give space to your sensations, thoughts, feelings, and the physical objects and events occurring around you. You can give space to whatever is appearing in your experience right now.

You are unlimited, aware space, so you don't need to pick and choose what you are aware of and what you allow into your experience. You can just give it all space to be here. Imagine if you were a multi-trillionaire. Having essentially limitless money would mean you could give lots of it away and still not run out. You are like a multi-multi-trillionaire when it comes to spacious awareness. You truly can't run out. You can give space to anything that shows up.

When you give space to your experiences, it shifts you more fully into the spaciousness of your Being, which is experienced in the Heart. You can imagine space flowing to or around the objects and sensations, or you can simply notice that there is already space for them. A simple test to determine if there is space for something is to notice if it exists: If something exists, there must be enough space for it to exist.

Exercise: *Experiment giving aspects of your experience space. Imagine space flowing to them or around them. Or simply notice that the objects and events around you and within you already do have enough space to exist. Give space to your body and sensations just as they are. Give space to* your thoughts, feelings, and desires. Give space to the objects in the room. Give space to the sounds appearing in your environment. Give lots of space to everything you can notice right now. What is that like? How spacious and free do you feel when you give space to everything?

There's no need to be stingy—give things as much space as they need and more. If some aspect of your experience seems difficult or uncomfortable, then give it lots and lots of space. What happens if you give that difficulty or discomfort all of the space in your neighborhood? How about if you give it as much space as the entire country you are in? Or all of the space in the world or the solar system? How important does it seem now? What else do you notice about that difficulty or discomfort when you are giving it lots of space?

It can be helpful to start experimenting with giving space to something neutral like a piece of furniture or the sounds of birds outside. Once you have a sense of your capacity to give space to your experiences, you can experiment with giving space to more challenging, difficult, or painful aspects of your life.

Don't worry too much about what it actually means to "give something space." Even if the experiment of giving space is mostly intellectual at first, it can still put you in touch with that space. And since that aware space is what you are, it also puts you more in contact with your true nature.

Much of the time we have a sense of being limited. It seems like there is only so much time and awareness available, so we feel the need to pick and choose what we give our awareness to. We try to withdraw awareness from events or circumstances we don't like or want and focus it on what we do want.

The key is to give space and awareness to everything. You can give space to *both* your thoughts *and* your sensations. You can give space to *both* an external event *and* the feelings it evokes within you. You can give space to *both* a sense of excitement *and* a sense of fear about the same event *and* any doubts or worries you have about it *and* any memories that get triggered *and* any insights that arise in the midst of all these other responses. You can always give space to this and that and everything else.

Exercise: *Notice something that is happening in your environment or, more generally, in your life right now. As you give space to this, also give space to the thoughts appearing in your mind about it. Simultaneously, give space to the feelings or desires you have about it. Give as much space as all of these events and internal reactions need and more. You can't run out of space. As you continue to give space to these things, also give space to everything else in your environment: other people, unrelated events and objects, and unrelated thoughts and feelings. Notice that you can just keep giving space to more and more of what makes up your life and experience. What is that like?*

Emptiness Knows Better Than You

Q: Teachers like you have such an iron, rock solid assuredness about the truth that I don't seem to share. I'm in a state of questioning, and you are not. I want this rock solid assuredness! Is there something I'm not getting? How come you have rock solid assuredness and I don't?

A: While I can't speak for other teachers, I can share my own experience and perspective. We often search for things like "rock solid assuredness" in the wrong place. We hope to find solidity and sureness in the outer world by becoming secure and safe through money and power, or we hope to find it in some final understanding or enlightenment. However, these things don't provide the sense of solidity, assuredness, or security we seek because both outer and inner experience is always changing.

The source of everything that matters, including a solid sense of connection to Being, is emptiness itself. Emptiness is at the core of everything, including our body and our awareness. Yet empty space doesn't seem like a very promising place to find anything solid! And it is not that emptiness is solid—emptiness has no qualities, which is why we call it emptiness. But while emptiness has no qualities, it does have an infinite capacity to express or create all the qualities of existence that really matter, like love, peace, joy, strength, clarity, compassion, and many more. These qualities are real and "solid." They have much more reality than our thoughts and mental images and even more reality than physical objects.

The challenge is that we never know what will arise out of emptiness in any particular moment, or if anything will arise at all. One moment you might experience a powerful sense of pure existence that is solid and more real than a mountain of stone arising out of the empty source of all experiences, and the next moment you might experience a sense of spacious, light joy that doesn't feel particularly solid but is still very real. And the next moment may just be empty beyond any concept of emptiness you can imagine.

What you are interpreting as rock solid assuredness in a teacher may instead be a deep sense of trust that whatever arises next will be fine. I don't ever know what is going to arise in the next moment, but I've developed a sense of trust that it will be fine whatever it is. Trust is subtly different from the rock solid assuredness you describe. Trust is more like a soft, warm, golden light that allows an open and totally accepting embrace of uncertainty and surprises. Trust is more subtle and yet more real than even experiences of certainty, which come and go. Trust is a fundamental quality that arises out of the emptiness from which everything else also arises.

Trust is gained from experience. We trust physical objects to behave a certain way because we have so much experience with them. The same can happen with the experience of your true nature. However, the trust of true nature is necessarily more subtle because true nature is infinitely varied in its expression. Yet this subtlety means that as your essential trust deepens, more and more can be included. Everything that has ever happened has come from your true nature expressing itself in all the dimensions of existence.

Deeply exploring, sensing, and understanding experiences that arise helps you develop this essential trust. All of your experiences are showing you something about your true nature. I invite you to make friends with your uncertainty and get to know it very well. Uncertainty is the lack of certainty, and the lack of anything is actually the experience of emptiness. Whenever it seems like something is missing, that is an experience of emptiness. It is an endless surprise to discover that the source of what seemed to be missing is found in that same feeling of lack or emptiness when you go more deeply into that sense of lack or emptiness. For example, any certainty, insight, or understanding you experience comes out of the sense of emptiness that your mind might label a lack of certainty. In fact, it is in the moments when we allow ourselves to not know that insight or knowing is most freely able to arise.

Trust is knowing that even when certainty is not here, the source of certainty is. And this is also the source of love, joy, curiosity, and everything else that really matters. The important thing is not an ongoing experience of solidity or assuredness or any other quality of Being but, rather, a trust that those qualities will arise when truly needed. Developing this trust requires endlessly letting go of any agenda for how life should feel or what should arise. That is how you discover that whatever is here can be trusted completely. The emptiness knows better than we do what is needed in this moment.

You Cannot Be Harmed

The following is from the free ebook That Is That *by Nirmala, which is available at http://endless-satsang.com/free*

Consciousness is affected by experience but not harmed. It is the nature of aware consciousness to be affected by everything it experiences. Every color and sound, every event and experience, and every passing thought or feeling affects your consciousness. A rock isn't as affected by these things, so we consider a rock less conscious than a person.

And yet, consciousness is not harmed by anything. Its nature is that it can't be harmed. The form of anything can be harmed or permanently changed. Your body can be harmed, for example, but the consciousness that contains your body cannot. Your consciousness is made of empty space, and that is the only indestructible thing there is.

This is good news. It's like a "Get out of Jail" card in Monopoly. No matter what happens, you, as aware space, are completely unharmed. What a relief! There's nothing that can harm you. No one and nothing has ever harmed you.

This is not to say that consciousness isn't affected deeply by both the good and bad things that happen to us. Every hurtful and unkind act leaves an impression in the consciousness of those involved. It's just that the impression doesn't permanently limit or damage the awareness of those involved. If something permanently affects us, it could be said to have harmed us. But if the effect is temporary, then what is the ultimate harm? Everything that profoundly affects our awareness, from the beautiful to the tragic, eventually passes. It is the miracle of our consciousness that it can heal from any wound, even if our body cannot.

What you are is eternal, aware space, or consciousness. You have a body, but you are not that body. So while your body can be permanently harmed, just like your car or camera can be, you, as consciousness, eventually heal or recover from every experience that has affected you. Even if the effect lasts for lifetimes, eventually it is diminished and disappears. From the perspective of something eternal, even many lifetimes isn't that long.

Realizing that your true nature as consciousness can't be harmed puts all of life's difficulties in perspective. Similarly, when someone's car is totaled in an accident but he or she isn't hurt, we consider that person lucky. This is because we have a perspective on the relative importance of damage to a car. It's not such a big deal relative to a serious physical injury or death. If you realize that you are aware space, then everything else is like the totaled car—no big deal.

Some things are still more important than others. Physical harm is still a bigger difficulty than harm to a car or other physical object. But by knowing that your true nature is space, which cannot harmed, the bigger difficulties and even tragedies in life can be seen in perspective.

A simple question to ask is, "What effect does this experience have on my eternal soul?" And while everything leaves an impression on your awareness and your soul, nothing can ever permanently harm your soul, your true nature as empty aware space. In fact, every experience enriches your soul. Every moment adds to the depth and richness of your deepest knowing. We sense this in people who've faced a lot of difficulty in life and who've accepted their fate. There's a depth and wisdom that only comes from a wide range of experience, including painful and unwelcome experiences.

The willingness to meet and have any experience comes from the recognition that what you are is open, spacious awareness. Your body, mind, personality, emotions, and desires all appear within that awareness, but they are not you. And the real you cannot be harmed.

Awareness Is Limitless: A Talk by Nirmala

An mp3 recording of a talk given in satsang is available to purchasers of this book at:

http://endless-satsang.com/part2mp3

Chapter 3

WISDOM

Wisdom, or discrimination, is another fundamental quality of our true nature. In every experience, there is awareness and space and also endless differences. No two experiences are the same, and the spacious awareness that you are notices the differences. Noticing differences is inherent in awareness because awareness notices what is, and what is, is always changing and therefore different: The temperature of the room is always changing, the sounds you hear are always new, and thoughts are never the same twice. Your true nature discriminates between all of these differences.

One of the most important distinctions our awareness is capable of is how true something is. Something that is very true is experienced differently than something that is not very true. The difference is that the bigger truth opens your Heart and expands your sense of yourself, while the smaller truth contracts your Heart and gives you a smaller sense of yourself. Discriminating in this way is as natural and effortless as distinguishing cold water from hot when you put your hands under a faucet. Contraction just happens when you encounter a smaller truth, and expansion or relaxation just happens when you encounter a bigger truth.

These expansions and contractions happen inside of you, to the sense of your Being. The challenge is that we often mistakenly conclude that we are small, inadequate, or unworthy whenever we contract; while actually the thought, feeling, belief, desire, or experience that is shaping our awareness in that moment is what is small, inadequate, and possibly unworthy. Understanding that you have this capacity for discrimination can turn your world inside out. How big or small you feel has nothing to do with you, but is simply a reflection of how big or small your experience is in the moment!

Discrimination is natural and inherent in your awareness. It's not something you need to do or get better at. But you can learn to pay more attention to the different ways your awareness feels and experiences life and your own Being. In particular, you can pay more attention to your capacity to know how true your thoughts, feelings, desires, and beliefs are.

The Heart's Wisdom

What follows is an excerpt from Living from the Heart *(to sample or purchase the book, go to http://endless-satsang.com/free), which introduces how to distinguish how true something is:*

The truth is that which opens the Heart. The capacity to sense the truth is something we all already have. We all have a Heart that is already accurately showing us how true things are. Anything that puts you in touch with more of the truth opens the Heart. This is a literal and experiential description of truth. When your experience is bringing you more truth, there is a sense of opening, softening, relaxation, expansion, fulfillment, and satisfaction in the Heart. This can be most directly sensed in the center of the chest, but the Heart of all Being is infinite and therefore actually bigger than your entire body. So this opening, softening, and expansion is actually happening everywhere; we just sense it most clearly and directly in the center of the chest.

When you encounter truth, the sense of your self opens, expands, softens, fills in, and lets go. The *me*, the sense of your self, is no longer felt to be so limited or small. It becomes more complete and unbounded. The boundaries soften and dissolve, and any sense of inadequacy, limitation, or deficiency is lessened or eliminated.

A side effect of being in touch with more of the truth is that your mind gets quieter, because you have less to think about. Even knowing a simple truth, like where your car keys are, gives you less to think about. And when you touch upon a very large truth, your mind becomes even quieter, like when you see the ocean for the first time: The truth or reality you're viewing is so immense that, at least for a moment, your mind is stopped and becomes very quiet.

In contrast, when your experience is moving into a diminished or smaller experience of the truth and of reality, the Heart contracts. The sense of your self gets tight, hard, contracted, and feels incomplete, bounded, and limited. It can feel like you are small, inadequate, or unworthy. The smallness of the truth is reflected in the smallness of the sense of your self. The result of being less in touch with the truth is that your mind gets busier as it tries to figure out what is true.

Fortunately, your Being is never diminished or contracted, only the *sense* of your self. Just as blocking your view of the whole room by partially covering your eyes makes your sense of the room smaller without actually making the room smaller, an idea or belief that is not very true is reflected in a small sense of your self, without actually limiting or contracting your Being.

This opening and closing of the Heart in response to the degree of truth you are experiencing isn't something you need to practice or perfect. Your Heart has been accurately and perfectly showing you how true your experience has been all along. If you start to notice your Heart's openings and closings, you'll discover that you already have everything you need to determine what is true. The Heart is the true inner teacher, the source of inner guidance we all have as our birthright. You don't need a spiritual teacher or spiritual books to show you what is true, just your own Heart.

Truth is what exists, what is here now. So if what exists is also what is true, then there is only truth. Whatever is present is true—but to varying degrees. There is no falsehood or untruth, only varying degrees of the truth.

We are always experiencing the truth. But because we don't experience everything in any one moment, our experience of truth is always limited. Sometimes we experience a large amount of truth—of what is actually here—and sometimes we experience only a small amount of what is actually happening, of what is true. Our Heart's openness or lack of openness in each moment shows us how much of the truth is being experienced in any moment.

What about ideas that are mistaken? An idea or belief that has little or no correspondence to external reality is going to be an extremely small truth, so small it may only exist in one person's mind, like the saying: "He was a legend in his own mind." When you experience an erroneous idea or belief, your Heart will contract appropriately to show you that that idea or belief is a very small truth.

For example, if you entertain the idea that you will never be happy unless you have ten million dollars, your Heart will contract appropriately to show you that that is just an idea with very little truth. This contraction may be so quick that it doesn't cause you any suffering or trouble. But if you really believe this idea, the sense of your self will contract for as long as that idea is held. Another example is the idea that it is better to be thinner, more beautiful, or younger than you are. This is a smaller truth than the idea that you are perfect the way you are. If you believe this smaller truth, the sense of your self will contract—you will suffer. Even if you *are* beautiful, thin, or young, the idea that it is better to be that way than the opposite can limit the sense of your self. If it's better to be that way, you can't just relax and be. You will probably feel like you need to do something to stay that way.

In contrast, a neutral idea that doesn't state or imply anything about you can be experienced neutrally in your sense of self. For example, if you consider the color of the ceiling in someone's house, this usually won't open or close your Heart because it's not about you and probably doesn't imply anything about you. The sense of your self doesn't shift in response to neutral ideas like this.

Thoughts are real—they exist—but they exist only as ideas. You could put all the thoughts ever thought into a pile, and they still wouldn't trip anybody. They only exist as neural firings in the brain, so to focus on thoughts exclusively is to severely limit or contract your experience of reality and therefore the sense of your self.

In the range of everyday experience, our ideas have varying degrees of correspondence with reality. Ideas that correspond more closely to reality won't contract or limit the sense of self for as long as mistaken ones. Many ideas are of service to our ability to be at ease in the world. For example, when you need to go someplace, correct ideas about how to get there allow you to go there and then move on to other experiences. Ideas such as these can enhance our experience rather than limit or contract it. An idea about where something is located is, of course, not a big truth, but it's also not usually experienced as limiting.

All there is, is truth, and our Heart's capacity to reflect the degree of truth in any experience is the way we recognize how true a particular experience is.

What is this Heart? What is this sense of self that is ever present? It doesn't relate to sensations in the physical heart or chest. It's a more subtle sense, at times even more subtle than the physical senses, although the opening or contracting can also be experienced as relaxation and contraction in the physical body. The sense of your self, the sense that you exist, is something more intimate than your physical experience.

What does it mean when you say *me*? What are you referring to when you say *me*? This simple fact that we are here, that we exist, is a very mysterious aspect of our experience. When we speak of it poetically to try to capture its essence, we call it the Heart, like when you know something in your Heart or when your Heart is touched.

This sense of your self is a very alive and changing experience. At times, your sense of self is open, free-flowing, and expanded. At other times, like when a judgment arises, your sense of self feels small, inadequate, and deficient. In these moments, have you actually changed? Has your body suddenly shrunk? Much of the time this sense of self is bigger than or smaller than your physical body. How does that work? Have you ever experienced your inner child? How can your sense of self be the size of a child when you are an adult? The sense of self is shifting all the time. It's always either opening and expanding, or contracting and tightening, similar to the ongoing expansion and contraction of our breathing.

This opening and closing of the Heart is not a prescription—something you need to practice—but simply a description of what your Heart has been doing your entire life. Whatever does happen in the sense of self in any moment is entirely correct and appropriate. It's appropriate for your Heart to close when someone is telling you a small, limiting truth; and it's appropriate for your Heart to open when you experience a deep and profound reality.

The Contracted Heart

Q: I don't seem to be able to find what expands my Heart. I feel so stuck. It's all so dry.

A: Trusting the Heart is particularly challenging when you feel contracted and dry. But that is the right way for a small or incomplete perspective to feel. When life seems off purpose and there is no Heart resonance with what is happening, the invitation is to be with the experience of contracted dryness just as it is. Sometimes it just isn't time for the truer direction to appear, as the bigger mystery often has its own timing, which doesn't always fit with our agenda. Sometimes there is something more to be seen about our resistance and conditioning, and often we are only willing to look at our conditioning when that conditioning is no longer working for us. The dryness and difficulty may get us to finally pay attention to something that needs to be seen.

When the Heart is contracted, it is still working perfectly to show you the nature of your experience. The real art of inquiry is to give space and curiosity to the tightness itself, instead of trying to push through to a bigger truth. Our conditioned reactions are showing up to be seen, accepted, and loved. Once this conditioning is seen, it naturally falls into proper perspective. These small truths don't need to be gotten rid of, but just seen as small. There's room in our awareness and in our Heart for all of life's experiences, including very small and limited perspectives.

While questioning the truth of our limited or stuck places may be challenging, doing so can also be profoundly liberating. The discovery that even an experience of dryness and stagnation is something to be valued and explored frees us from the compulsion to try to fix or change our experience. There are insights and treasures to be found in every aspect of our experience. We can explore our experience, not to get a better one, but to fully taste and digest the treasures found in every experience.

The Heart's Wisdom in Relationships

Q: *When my Heart contracts in response to another person's words, is that a sign of how true the other person's words are or a sign of how true something is that is being triggered inside of me?*

A: One of the challenging things about our inner knowing is that it responds instantly to whatever is in awareness in a particular moment, and that's always changing. So in interactions with others and in response to your own thoughts or insights, you are likely to experience a variety of expansions and contractions as words are spoken, thoughts and feelings arise, and conditioned reactions are triggered. For example, while someone is criticizing you, your Heart is likely to contract in response to the relative truth of their criticism. And if, in the next moment, you think, "They're right. I'm a jerk," your Heart might contract even more. In contrast, if you compassionately think, "Oh, he just lost his job, so he's probably in a bad mood today," this wider perspective might start your Heart opening. So the responses of your Being are as fast as thought, and we can have a lot of thoughts in a very short time. Your Heart is always responding to the words as they are spoken or the thought or reaction you are having in that instant.

When it comes to relationships, it can be hard to catch what is true and what isn't, as there are often so many reactions in both people that are being expressed both verbally and nonverbally, and your Heart is responding to each one, even if only for an instant. That's why I often say it matters more what the overall climate of a relationship is like than what the weather is like today. The question is, in the midst of triggering each other all day long, are there also moments of truly expanded love and joy? Which is predominant? The joy and love in just a moment of true Heart connection and celebration can be enough to counterbalance a lot of petty annoyances that may also be a part of being together.

If you are always contracting when someone does something, it might be your Heart's accurate response to the truth of their actions. The question really is what happens in the next moment. Do you "get the joke" that it isn't very true and just laugh it off and move on, or are you still thinking about it an hour later? If the latter, then you probably need to take a look at your own conditioning. But that doesn't mean that if that person is repeatedly triggering you all day long there isn't something in him or her that also needs to be seen for what it is. You are under no obligation to stay around someone who continually acts without integrity or awareness.

We can also use the Heart in making choices about practical matters, such as where to live or whether to stay in a job. What matters is the overall sense over time regarding a specific direction, not just how your Heart is responding in a particular moment. So when it comes to major decisions, it's best to take some time sensing the overall climate of your being's responses to the various options and to your reactions to the various options and any ramifications of each option that you can think of before deciding. At some point, there will be enough evidence in your Heart to know the relative merit of the various options. By the way, your Heart is still working fine if it registers no real difference between the options. That probably just means that whatever you choose in that situation doesn't really matter!

The Beginning That Never Happened to the End That Never Comes

Q: I feel small and what worries me is that it's hard to tolerate all that is happening when the context of enlightenment is disappearing. What's happening is just happening, and to see it as happening for a purpose doesn't make sense. It seems to be calling for some real humbleness... and even that isn't something I can do. It seems that the teaching of allowing is all that's left, and yet I have nothing good to show for it. So there's doubt about it. Can this be over some day?

A: If you're feeling small, then your awareness is working perfectly. Fear and doubt are supposed to feel that way. Imagine if your body could be any size depending on what clothes you put on: If you put on baby clothes, you would be very small. If you put on a doll's clothes, you would be even smaller. And if you put on a giant's clothes, you would suddenly be huge. Awareness is like that. When you experience a small, limiting perspective like fear, doubt, or a desire, then your awareness contracts to fit into it. And when you are struck by a profound truth, your awareness opens into a larger field. Your awareness is working perfectly when you feel small. This isn't a sign of anything wrong. And, of course, your awareness is also working fine when it opens up wide.

By the way, ideas about enlightenment tend to be as small as any other idea or belief. There's nothing special about concepts about enlightenment. They are small truths, but they can sometimes function as pointers to a bigger truth, such as the enlightened nature of your awareness just as it is right now.

As you pointed out, the challenge is that it's not up to you how big the truth of each moment is. There's a dance between the bigger truth of your Being and the smaller truths of your conditioning. You don't choose which one is happening, but you can learn to trust your awareness to show you which one is happening. Then, when a small truth arises, you recognize that it's small and hold it lightly. And when a big truth arises, you recognize that it's a profound truth and celebrate it while it lasts.

This is the way your awareness has been working all along. Your awareness has always been showing you, moment to moment, how big or small some truth is. Experiencing a big truth isn't better except that the expansion shows you how big your experience of awareness can be (and how big the nature of awareness is). If you simply trust the smallness of your Being when that is what's happening, you won't suffer in the midst of that contraction. However, if you resist or struggle against the contraction, it tends to last longer.

Your awareness has always been working perfectly. Contraction is as natural to awareness as it is to your muscles. Contraction will never be over, and it doesn't need to be over. Awareness loves the endless journey of its existence from the beginning that never happened to the end that never comes.

The Truth Has Got a Hold of Us

Q: I'm confused over knowing when my intuitions are true and when the ego is imitating my intuition. It makes it hard to decide what to do. Maybe it doesn't matter what you do, but it feels like it does.

A: The truth not only has many levels, but these levels are all operating at the same time. So when you have an intuition and follow it, that may be essence working through you to create a certain experience in line with a deeper wisdom and your life purpose. At the same time, your ego will either resist that intuition and try to block you or decide it likes that intuition and maybe even take credit for it! The ego can interfere with an intuition or even mix things up by trying to make something happen that the ego thinks should happen in relation to that intuition.

What you do or where you end up obviously matters on a relative level, but the even bigger truth is that the empty, spacious awareness that is experiencing all of this can't be harmed no matter what you do. Wherever you end up and whatever happens, the empty space of Being will be just as empty and just as aware.

Realizing this bigger truth is likely to affect the unfolding of the smaller truths of both intuition and egoic agendas. For example, knowing that you can't be harmed might make it possible to risk following your intuition or even risk indulging in a particularly irresistible egoic desire. It's like gambling with someone else's money—what do you have to lose?

The truth isn't something we can grasp, define, or get a hold of. It might be more accurate to say that the truth has a hold on us and is playing us like a maestro plays the orchestra: a little more brass here, a little less ego there. The mind tries to find some kind of meaning in or explanation for all of this. The Heart knows that love never gets meaning from life, but gives meaning to life. And like any truly creative process, the results are always a wonderful surprise, even to the creator!

Inquiry into the truth isn't meant to be a way to finally get it or get somewhere, but a way to uncover ever bigger mysteries. What an amazing journey it has always been.

Inner vs. Outer Guidance

Q: Can I trust my inner sense of fullness to guide me more than outer signs and coincidences?

A: You can trust that inner fullness much more than any external signs. The challenge is to trust that inner fullness even when it seems to not be there. When you feel empty or contracted, that is also your inner guidance operating. Like the kid's game, where someone tells you you're getting warmer or colder in pointing you in a certain direction, so you need the moments of feeling dry and contracted to let you know you are "getting colder."

However, the really wonderful thing about listening inside is not that it gets you somewhere—to the right place or to where you want to go—but rather that it brings you to the fullness of your Being that is already here right now. It turns out that it doesn't matter that much what happens in life or whether you make the right or wrong choice. What matters are the rich, endless mysteries to be found in the *awareness* that notices what happens. The value in paying attention to an inner sense of fullness is not where it leads you, but simply what it shows you about yourself right now. You are a limitless source of everything that really matters: peace, joy, and love. All this is available right now and in every moment, even if you end up taking the wrong bus to nowhere!

Letting Small Truths Be Small

Q: *What I'm wanting to achieve is a continued immersion of love. I write about very positive ideas, but all the problems of the day are still in my mind. My usual state is separate from the enlightened state I'm in when I'm writing. How do I integrate these two states?*

A: The big truths and the small truths of your life are all true. The difference is in how important and meaningful you take them to be. So if a small truth or problem arises in your mind, the right way to feel is contracted. That's how you know that that idea or problem isn't very important. That "problem" may still need to be addressed in some way, although sometimes when a truth is very small, it also means there's nothing you need to do about it. You don't need to integrate the small truths and the big truths; you just need to see them for what they are. They all already fit perfectly in the infinite space of your awareness.

Paradoxically, it is by allowing the small truths and recognizing their smallness that we are freed from any suffering they may cause. In fact, it is our struggle to change them or get rid of them that causes us to suffer or feel less immersed in love. In trying to change these small truths, we get temporarily stuck in them. In allowing them, our awareness is freed to move outside, or beyond, the smaller truth they contain. And it is often then that the solutions to them become obvious.

This is backwards from how we think it should work. Trying to get more of the expanded, loving feeling actually contracts us. Wanting to be expanded contracts us! This is simply because it isn't very true that it's better to be expanded. The ideal is to experience each moment the way it really is. A small truth should feel small because that's how you can tell how important it is.

You can still enjoy the expanded, loving moments, of course. However, the bigger freedom is when it doesn't matter anymore whether you're expanded or contracted. Contracting doesn't mean you have lost the capacity to expand; it just means that in this moment something is shaping and limiting your awareness. In allowing and embracing the full range of your awareness, you are able to respond to each moment just as it is without needing to feel any way in particular.

It turns out that this accepting, allowing way of being does actually lead to more expanded experiences. The default is for your awareness to expand and your Heart to open. By letting everything unfold just as it does, you naturally fall into this default position more often. But the expansion just happens. You never actually do it, and anything you do to try to make it happen tends to have the opposite effect.

I will add a small tip: If you find yourself struggling with a problem, the first step is to allow your struggling and the contraction it causes. That's what then enables you to move into allowing the problem itself. You can only start with what's happening right now, and sometimes what's happening is that you don't like what's happening. In simply meeting any resistance that is here right now, you open the door for the bigger truths of love, compassion, and understanding to flow into your experiences of struggle and difficulty.

Decisions Are Not That Important

Q: *I'm still grappling with the relative importance or truth of my fears and projections. For example, if a job comes my way and I feel contracted about it, I don't know whether that contraction is because of feedback from the Heart ("Not much truth here for you") or arising from a fear of change ("I'll have to move") or from old wounds ("Poverty is more comforting and familiar"). Here's another example: Someone invites me to dinner, and although my mind is saying, "Yes, yes, what fun," my chest is saying, "No way." This could be Heart guidance or some aversion or fear.*

A: The art is to catch what is happening right as the contraction starts. Are you purely thinking of taking the new job? Or are you thinking a judgmental or fearful thought about it? Some of our thoughts are so automatic that they are almost unconscious. Catching what is actually happening in awareness at the exact moment of the contraction can be challenging. So in making big decisions, it helps to slow down, take one possibility at a time, and also give yourself lots of time to see what the overall climate of truth is regarding that decision.

When it comes to practical decisions and sorting through the many thoughts, feelings, intuitions, desires, longings, and impulses of our daily life, there are limitations to how useful the Heart can be. That's because it often doesn't matter that much what we decide and what we do each moment. Our decisions are often not that important. From the perspective of our soul, it may not be a big deal where we work or live or what we do, although the Heart will still register a relative difference between any two possibilities if there is one (sometimes two choices are equally true).

The real value of listening to your Heart moment to moment is not that it makes everything work out well and avoids all pitfalls and wrong turns, but that it means that you are listening when a profound truth arises. When you are touched by a deeper knowing, the Heart shows you how true the bigger truth is by softening and expanding to a striking degree. You can expand right out of your usual sense of "me." These bigger truths appear in our lives spontaneously and more often than we might realize, so it is a great gift when we are present and aware of them.

Our Inner Compass Is Always Working

Q: *I've been reading lately about how certain childhood experiences result in "addiction to unhappiness," that is, the inner compass of what feels right is off. So self-sabotage and veering toward situations that don't serve occur. If this is true, the Heart is off, and you're at sea without a compass.*

A: I don't agree that the Heart can be wounded in a way that causes the inner compass to be off. Even when there is an unconscious addiction to unhappiness, the Heart still shows you how true your addictions or compulsions are. Your inner compass still works even if you aren't following it but, instead, following a false compass, such as your fears or desires.

Of course, we are often rewarded for our addictive behavior with a pleasurable or comforting sensation or emotion, a false sense of superiority, or protection against our own self judgment, but that isn't actually an expanded and easeful experience. I often say the truth feels like when you have a roommate and he or she goes away for a month—you can just relax and be yourself. Our addictive and distorted defense mechanisms never result in that sense of just being able to be yourself. They are more like your roommate coming back and bringing his or her parents for a month-long visit: You can't just relax and be. When we are involved in our defense mechanisms, we can never relax and just be; we always have to keep up our defenses.

Because consciousness has no preferences, it allows you to move into any experience, including contracted, confused defenses against the residue of childhood wounding. Consciousness is also always willing to see the truth of that wounding and thereby start to heal it in a way that actually does allow an expansion and realization of our truer nature.

The Radio of the Mind

Q: *What if thoughts don't come from us but to us, the brain being like an advanced radio, tuning in to a field of potential thought? What if thoughts are reading us as much as we are reading them? What if thoughts are aware? Would knowing this change our thinking and our attitude toward thoughts? Would it change our thoughts' attitude toward us?*

A: My sense is that thoughts and also intuitions and insights come from many different sources, and the mind is like a radio that picks them all up. Many of the thoughts our mind picks up are simply triggered from our memory, and so often they are of limited helpfulness in understanding this new moment. Some people are very sensitive and their "radio" even picks up other people's thoughts, which may or may not be relevant to their experience. And then there are thoughts, or insights, that come to us from deeper dimensions of our being. These can sometimes be profoundly helpful and liberating in the moment that they appear.

So how do we tune the "radio" of our mind to a useful and liberating station? It seems the mind just picks up all of the stations and plays every thought that arises. So perhaps the best we can do is to clearly discriminate between conditioned thoughts that come to us from memory and the deeper knowings that also appear in our awareness. By sorting out whether a particular thought or insight is very true or not, the various bits and pieces of information and intuition that appear in our minds are put into perspective. The important thing is to recognize how true our experiences are, including our thoughts and intuitions.

As for thoughts themselves being aware, I would say that everything is alive and aware and affected by everything else. However, just as some things are more true than others, some forms of life have more awareness. Obviously a human has more awareness than a bug, and the bug has more awareness than an amoeba. My sense is that thoughts are like incredibly small bugs with a very short life span. They hatch, mate, and die in a flash. See if you can find the thought you were just having, or do you need to think a new thought? So even if a thought has awareness, it doesn't exist long enough as a separate form to evolve or be affected by much.

I hold all ideas lightly, and yet the biggest truth is that there is just one awareness here. All of the forms and identities that appear, from thoughts to bugs to human beings to galaxies, are temporary expressions of this one awareness that is dreaming (thinking?) them all into existence. What a beautiful dream it is!

True Healing

Q: I'm dealing with a severe illness. I inquired and found that I have little or no will to live, that I fear God is punishing me with this illness, and that I also feel I don't deserve to be healed or have a passionate, full life. I sense that I need to heal my lack of a will to live before I can heal my disease.

A: I'm very impressed with the depth and honesty of your inquiry. It does seem that to heal your physical illness, you must first "heal" the issue of your will to live. In this case, the deepest healing is the recognition that there is nothing to heal. By that I mean that there's nothing wrong or bad here, and you have done nothing wrong. It is simply not your fault that you feel this way but the fault of your conditioning, which is based on your actual life experiences. And your conditioning is not your fault.

Everything you've done in this life has been the best way you knew to take care of yourself. How can that be wrong? How can you judge someone for that or ever consider punishing them? (Note: I'm not saying it is never true for society to protect itself by jailing someone; it just doesn't make sense to punish people for acts that aren't their fault, which is probably why punishment rarely heals or rehabilitates anyone.)

If God is a halfway decent version of a god, he/she would know this. A real and worthy God is never judgmental and would never even consider punishing someone. If there is a god that does any of that, then I say it is time to get a new God and fire the old one! Fortunately, all we have to change is our belief about God, since the reality is that God, or True Being, never judges or punishes.

You deserve and have always deserved to live, love, be loved, have a passionate life with people you enjoy, and live wherever you wish. The first step is to continue exploring your beliefs. You can also send these beliefs the same healing energy you might send to others or your own body. Maybe you could put your hands on your head and send healing energy to your beliefs, your guilt, and the whole package of conditioning. You don't have to get rid of those beliefs. Since belief is just a habitual thought and you can't get rid of your potential to think something, all you need to do is love your beliefs, let them be here, and see that they are not very true.

The important thing is to see that your thoughts are not very true. The truth is whatever opens your Heart and quiets the mind. Any thought or belief you uncover that has the opposite effect on your Heart and mind is simply not very true. That belief isn't wrong or bad or even false, but just a very small expression of the truth trying to act as if it were a big truth, like a little child trying to act big and strong. You can just love that belief for the truth it does have and invite it to relax and rest from trying so hard to be a big truth. There's room in your awareness for all of the truths, no matter how big or small, for all of the thoughts and all of the fears. But you can also see these thoughts as they are and see that they are not very true. This is what heals beliefs—simply seeing them as they really are.

Seeing the whole truth of any dis-ease or difficulty is the healing of it—seeing the conditioning behind it, seeing the nature of the sensations your body is having, and also seeing your beliefs and conditioning about the difficulty. What is actually true right now? These sensations are here, but what is true about them? Are they really bad sensations. or are they just particular sensations? Are your fears about them very true? Is the love that can still flow through your hands and your heart to your own body very true?

The only trick to all of this is to start where you are. If right now you don't want to live, then that's what you need to explore and love and allow. You don't have to get rid of the feeling that you don't want to live, just explore it as it is. How true is that feeling? What happens if you just let it be here? What else do you feel? What else is true? You don't need to change how you feel or get rid of any feeling, just find out everything you can about each and every feeling. This isn't an attempt to get rid of anything, but an inquiry out of curiosity and love for these strange and miraculous things called feelings. These feelings are arising here in you to be seen and loved, not to be fixed or gotten rid of.

Less Than Half Isn't Nothing!

I often get questions about the contradictions in various spiritual teachings and even within a particular spiritual teaching, not to mention the contradictions in life itself! These seeming contradictions can be very confusing to the mind, as the mind has a hard time with opposite things both being true. However, life doesn't limit itself to what the mind can understand, and so life is perfectly fine with two opposite things both having some truth.

Whenever anyone writes or speaks (even spiritual teachers), they are at best speaking half of the truth. This is due to the limitation inherent in words. Much of the time, what we say contains much less than half of the truth. So when you read words that seem contradictory from different spiritual teachers or even from the same spiritual teacher, this is because it's often necessary to contradict yourself to fully express the truth. There are many levels, dimensions, and perspectives within consciousness, and they are all valid.

The real gift of any teaching is when it points out the part of the truth that hasn't been seen or is being overlooked. When someone discovers the part of the truth that they hadn't previously seen, they naturally want to hang onto it and even deny or reject the opposite truth. However, as challenging as this may be to accept, dualistic teachings are correct, teachings of pure nonduality are correct, and everything else is also correct to a greater or lesser degree. Just to be clear, some things are true, but not very true. So although very narrow, bigoted perspectives may have a tiny piece of truth, that doesn't make them important or very helpful or worthwhile. An example of something that is true but not very true is a lottery ticket: It's true that you can win if you buy a lottery ticket, but it's not very true. In fact, it is a ridiculously small truth!

What really matters is whether someone's words expand your own experience of the truth or not. Anything that adds to or expands your experience of truth opens and softens your Heart, quiets your mind, and expands your sense of yourself. So when words do this, you can savor them and ponder them to fully absorb what they are pointing to. If anyone's words (even a spiritual teacher's) have the opposite effect and contract your Heart, make your mind busy, and make you feel small or inadequate, then you know those words are not important for you. You don't need to reject them or make them wrong, just let the idea be there and move onto something that is truer for you.

The Experiential Qualities of Truth: A Talk by Nirmala

An mp3 recording of a talk given in satsang is available to purchasers of this book at:

http://endless-satsang.com/part3mp3

Chapter 4

DESIRE AND SUFFERING

Our true nature is an open, spacious, aware, Presence that is completely wise, discriminating, and alive. So why don't we experience our true nature all of the time? Why does it often seem that we are much less than our true potential?

This spacious awareness that you are can be shaped, and one of the most powerful shapers of your awareness is desire. Desire is a thought that has a direction to it, and usually that direction is away from where you already are. As your awareness follows a desire, your sense of yourself gets very contracted and tight, and the discomfort of the contraction adds to the illusion that you would be happier if you had what you desire. This movement of desire is the source of suffering. Suffering is, very simply, the gap between where our attention is flowing and where we already are. This gap, or difference between what we are giving our attention or awareness to and what is actually here, creates inner tension and discomfort. It is the source of all of our suffering and discomfort.

When, instead, our attention and awareness are flowing freely to whatever is already happening, we experience more of the qualities of our true nature, such as peace, joy, and love, and we experience less suffering. This is simply because the peace, joy, and love are found within our true nature and don't come from outer objects and experiences. So when our awareness is flowing freely and fully, we experience more peace and happiness.

Unfortunately, when we do pursue a desire and finally get something we want, our awareness naturally relaxes and flows more freely because we are no longer wanting. I say "unfortunately" because this tends to reinforce the misunderstanding that getting what we want makes us happy. If you feel happy every time you get something you want, it is natural to conclude that happiness comes from getting what you want. However, happiness can also arise anytime we are simply not wanting anything other than what is already here. The source of happiness is in spacious awareness, and this becomes obvious whenever we are not wanting anything other than what is already here. The source of happiness is in the flow of awareness, not in anything we just got. Why not go directly to the source of happiness instead of making happiness conditional on getting what you want?

There's nothing wrong with wanting or with getting what you want, but excessively focusing on what you want and the effortful contraction of awareness that is needed to maintain such a focus is the source of suffering. This is good news because it means that ending suffering is much simpler than you might have thought. You don't need to get what you want, and you don't even need to get rid of your desires. You just need to pay more attention to the source of your desires and the source of your awareness and pay less attention to your desires. When we give our awareness to what is already here, including the mysterious wonders of our true nature, the effort and contraction of suffering naturally relaxes.

The trick to not suffering over desires is to simply pay attention to the *experience* of desiring and to any suffering you are experiencing whenever you're desiring something. Right now, if suffering is here, pay attention to it. What is your suffering actually

Desire and Suffering

like? What is the energy of desire itself? Are the sensations of wanting actually bad sensations? How do you know you are wanting something? How do you know what you want? Are you suffering over your desire? How do you know you are suffering? Are the sensations of contraction or suffering actually bad sensations?

As you pay more attention to the actual experience of desire and suffering instead of giving your attention to the object of your desire, the flow of awareness that this allows fills in the gap that was causing you to suffer. What a surprise it is to find the end of suffering in the experience of suffering itself! It is the best kind of healing when you discover that there is nothing that needs to be healed. The best result when you go to the doctor is when he or she tells you that nothing is wrong and you are already healthy as can be. This is what happens when you pay more attention to your desire and suffering: You discover there is nothing wrong with desire or with suffering and that you can have all of your desires as long as you give this fullness of attention to the entire experience of desiring. Doing this is much easier than trying to satisfy all of your desires so that you can relax and be happy. Why not just be happy now?

Desiring What Is

The following is from Nothing Personal *by Nirmala. A longer excerpt of this book is available at http://endless-satsang.com/free*

The Buddha spoke about desire. He said that desire is the cause of all suffering—the root of all suffering. Desire is a very juicy word. It's got to be if it's going to have that much power that it can cause all of the suffering in the world. He didn't say most of the suffering or a lot of the suffering, but all of it—every single contraction of being is caused simply by desire. So, it's a very powerful force. So, it's worth looking into this thing that can cause all of the suffering you have ever experienced.

One of the things you can notice about desire—a very obvious thing that gets overlooked—is that every desire is a lie. Every desire is based on the idea that things can be different than they are, and that's just never been true. Things have never been different than they are in that moment. You can even see how this lie might come to be because things almost always are different than they were, but they just are never different than they are. They are always the way they are. So, in observing this, we start to think that we can take this constantly changing "the way things are" and decide how it's going to be next. That's also based on a lie. You can just look in your own experience. How often has it worked? How often have things turned out exactly the way you wanted them to be, the way you desired them to be? Unfortunately, every now and then it happens, so we get hooked—like with a slot machine. Every now and then we get what we desired. But it's a matter of random luck. If you desire enough things, every now and then you're going to get it right.

What people often do when they see this lie is accept the way things are. It's funny, though, in plain old acceptance there can be a sense of being defeated—a sense of resignation: I'll accept what is, but I don't have to like it! There can be that quality to acceptance. So, I invite you to consider another possibility. It's a strange possibility, but it's actually very wonderful in its results. And that is to actually desire *what is*: Meet what is with that same passion that you may have had for what could be or what you think should be happening. Meet what is with that kind of passion, with that force that is able to generate all the suffering in the world. Bring that force to bear on what is—on the truth instead of on a lie.

There's another word for this: gratitude. It's different than just accepting. Accepting is somehow lifeless; it lacks passion or juice. That's why even though people may get that things are the way they are, they often go back to the juice of wanting things to be different. At least in desiring there's drama, there's intensity, passion, and life, even if it does result in suffering. But there is this other possibility: actually desiring *what is* wholeheartedly, really truly saying yes to this moment, to what is, exactly the way it is right now, bringing that kind of passion and aliveness to the way things are. This brings instant unlimited happiness because every desire is fulfilled.

The reason that people don't make this simple but radical choice to want what is, is because it's so simple. You don't even have to raise a finger. Nothing is needed. People shy away from this because in wanting *what is*, the job description of the ego becomes "do nothing." There just really isn't anything left to do for the ego, for who you thought you were. That's the price to be paid: To truly want what is, you have to give up the idea of being someone who can change what is. There's no longer a place for that. Changing anything would be working at cross-purposes to what you desire.

Then you come up against this inescapable paradox that even your desire for things to be different than they are is something that you need to desire as it is. You can't leave that out. You can't leave out these desires that rise up—for a relationship or for money or for spiritual awakening or for the Truth. You have to meet those with this same gratitude. To realize that your own suffering has to be met with gratitude totally breaks open your heart.

Often when people are on a spiritual path, seeking the Truth, it's just another more subtle, sophisticated, dressed-up desire because the Truth is right here, right now. No seeking is required. The Truth has never been anywhere but right here, right now. People who are seeking the Truth are really seeking after a better truth than the one they've got. It's another form of desire. The invitation is to meet even that desire with gratitude. You have to desire to want the Truth if that is what is happening, even though wanting it is an impossibility and based on a lie. You still just open your arms and say yes.

You're never done. You're never done being grateful because *what is*, is always changing, always new. Every moment is fresh; it doesn't have any reference. It is a completely new chance to be grateful. Whatever is happening has never happened before—whatever emotions, thoughts, sensations, and experiences are happening are completely fresh and new right now. The opportunity to meet them with gratitude and passionately desire *what is*, is always available. You never run out of things to be grateful for.

There is an interesting thing that happens when you desire what is: you start to desire what will be. In desiring what is, you step into where it is going; you step into the flow, into this mysteriously unfolding, ever-new moment. This powerful force called desire can either cause all the suffering in the world or—

when turned to right here, right now—become this incredible power for flow, for beingness.

When that starts to happen, it is easy to get overly intrigued with that. It becomes this really fun thing—to apparently be manifesting something. It's actually a complete mystery how those two things are connected—your wanting something to happen and it happening. It would be just as accurate to say that it is a form of premonition. So, when that flow is happening, the temptation can be to get so intrigued with that, that you start to play with that. The second you get intrigued with how things are getting easier, it's like saying I'm grateful for the Truth as long as this flow-thing is happening. It's easy to be grateful when you're in the flow, and it's not that there's anything wrong with it. But if you get too interested in the flow and turn away from this mysterious meeting of the moment with gratitude, then your gratitude is no longer unconditional.

You have to be willing to throw your Heart open with gratitude even before there's any sense of the flow, to be willing to do that even when flow is a distant, vague memory. That's where the life is, that's where the juice is coming from, even this apparent flow. And the other thing about flow is that sometimes the shortest path between two points is through Hell, and that's the way flow is going to go sometimes. So, if you have the idea that flow looks like a flat tire being fixed really fast, you might discover that flow has a very different idea about how long you will be on the side of the highway and how late you will be to your next appointment.

It's not up to you how much suffering arises, which is devastating news to who you think you are if you are trying to get out of suffering. The good news is that it is up to something that is incredibly, profoundly wise, something that can see that the shortest path between two points goes through Hell sometimes.

And sometimes it goes through heaven. It has no preference. It just sees where this unfoldment needs to go right now, and it doesn't hold back. That's what has been happening all along. Has your life ever stopped unfolding in spite of how often it seems not to have gone where you wanted it to go? It still goes, right? Something is in there steering it, unfolding it.

It's not some Truth "out there" that we need to be grateful for, some Truth that will show up some time in the future. It's right here, right now—just exactly the way everything is right now. Nothing is left out. Recognizing that whatever is, is only here for this moment—it's only available in this moment and will never be available just this way again—gives us this juice, this passion to meet it with gratitude.

The reason we don't dive in with gratitude in moments of suffering or pain is because there is a mistaken attitude that if we do that, things will stay the same. We think that by loving this moment the way it is and all of its pain (if that's what is present), we will get stuck, when actually the opposite is true.

It makes sense for us to want to go to battle with our conditioning, which is behind our suffering, because our conditioning is so obviously a lie and it doesn't feel enlightened to have that conditioning, but when you fight it, it makes it seem really big. You've made it into something, as if it had anything to do with who you really are. On the other hand, if you take the perspective of desiring it instead of fighting it, you can see how ridiculous it is and laugh at it, and then it loses its potency. It is no longer a problem. It no longer controls you. It's just arising, and you're saying, "Great, wonderful, what a gas!" Then, it never even has a chance to turn into something called suffering. The event appears and the conditioned reaction to it appears, and a complete enjoyment of both happens, so any possibility of suffering is immediately swallowed. It's not like we are unfamiliar with this process; this happens whenever something goes right. Every moment can be like this, where everything shows up, but nothing is a problem. Then, nothing that happens controls you.

What cuts through any suffering is simply choosing *what is* in every moment. It's not some complicated formula. It's simply meeting what is with passion and gratitude. It really isn't up to you how many times your conditioning keeps appearing. If it were up to you, it would have been done a long time ago, right?

So the invitation is to find out for yourself what happens when you are willing to waste your desire on *what is*. Don't take my word for it. For just this moment, you can meet whatever is present with a passionate embrace. And then see if you can truly find any suffering here in this moment.

Surrender Is What Is

Q: I experience a looming hopelessness in ever truly fulfilling this yearning of totally surrendering to the Beloved. There is a resignation or a sense of, "What's the use?" Since I am not this body, what's the use of taking care of it?

A: Everything is unfolding naturally and normally. Within this unfolding, hopelessness is a valid perspective. However, I invite you to check if there is truly an absence of any hope or expectation, or if there is a negative expectation or negative hope that things will not unfold completely. True hopelessness is a recognition that there is no need for hope or expectation of any sort, since life itself brings every experience just as it is needed. It is hopeless for you to surrender only because you have already lost the struggle; life is already surrendering to itself. Everything is happening perfectly whether you struggle or not. At most, struggling delays things a bit and causes you to suffer, but it all works out anyway. So there's nothing you can do, nothing you need to do, and nothing you need to not do in order for surrender to happen. Surrender is not a prescription for you to follow, but a description of your true situation.

As for taking care of your body, while it ultimately doesn't matter if you don't take care of your body, it also doesn't matter if you take very good care of it. If you are meant to experience health and well-being, then life will bring these experiences to you. And if your soul chooses to experience physical challenges or diseases in this lifetime, then these will arise. Whatever experience is needed will naturally arise. Part of this natural arising is all that you do or don't do to take care of your body. If it truly doesn't matter, then it doesn't matter if you eat well, exercise, and get healing support for your body or if you don't. Holding the question this lightly allows deeper impulses and intuitions to guide you. It will simply feel truer in each and every moment to take care of the body or not to take care of the body. And this will change moment to moment as life unfolds. Sometimes you will be moved to take very good care of your body, and sometimes you will be moved to just let it be.

Sometimes, when we experience hopelessness and the depths of knowing that there is nothing we can do to fully surrender to Being, we fall into the trap of thinking that therefore we should do nothing. But there is also no non-doing that we can do to make surrender happen. It turns out that all of our doings and all of our non-doings are actually a part of the natural unfolding of life that already is coming from the surrendered depth of our soul.

In a scene in a Woody Allen movie, a UFO suddenly lands in front of him and little green men come out. Woody's character runs up to them and says, "Thank God you're here! What is the meaning of life? Is there a God? Why are we here?" And the little green men reply, "These are the wrong questions" and fly away again in their UFO, as Woody runs after them yelling, "Wait! What are the right questions?"

Sometimes the right question is not so much what should I do, but what is happening right now? What is this like? How do I know what I am thinking, feeling, or experiencing right now?" For instance, you might ask: "What's it like to have no hope or expectation either way? How do I know I am hopeless? What's it like to have a body right now? How do I know that this is my body? What is true right now? What am I spontaneously doing already? What is already surrendered to Being right now?"

This kind of inquiry is in between doing and non-doing. It isn't totally passive, but it isn't very active or effortful. It is giving space and curiosity to the unfolding of life that is already happening through you, around you, and within you. You can do this as hope comes and goes and as taking care of your body comes and goes. The real gift of this kind of questioning is not that it answers the more practical questions, but rather that it means you are paying attention when a bigger truth arises. If you are always asking, "What is happening right now?" then when a deep experience of Being arises, you'll notice. What a treasure it is to be home when the Beloved comes for a visit! Such questions don't make surrender happen, but they can show you that surrender is always here. Surrender is what is.

Following Desire Back to Its Source

Q: It often happens that I casually meet good-looking women during my day-to-day activities. As soon as this happens, something registers in my mind, and my equilibrium and tranquility are gone. I believe my thoughts and give attention to them, trying in every way to explore the situation. For hours and days to come, thoughts about that situation come back over and over again, even if the real situation is long gone. It seems I'm unable or I don't want to turn my attention beyond them to the present moment, to my looking Presence.

A: Your experience of being caught up in thought is a very common one. The mind is structured to focus in this way. The antidote is not to change or fix your thoughts, but to experience them even more fully and inquire: How do you know what you are thinking? What is thought, really? What is the benefit or reward you experience from these thoughts? What happens if you just let your thoughts be the way they are? What else is present right now besides thoughts? If you experience your thoughts more fully, it becomes easier to experience everything else that is also present more fully.

It's great that you have enough distance from your thoughts that they don't control your behavior. That distance allows you to not act on the thoughts if they aren't really true for you. By the way, there's nothing wrong with acting on a thought or an attraction to a woman if it is true for you to do so within the context of your life and the particular situation. But when it is not true to act on a thought, then that is an opportunity to explore thought and the nature of your mind.

One way to discover more about the nature of your thoughts is to drop down into the Heart or belly and experience your thoughts from there. This can naturally provide more distance from your thoughts and make it easier to observe their nature as well as experience more of the rest of reality. There's nothing wrong with thoughts, but they are a very small and limited aspect of reality. When we experience thoughts from the head, the thoughts are magnified and made to appear much bigger and more important than they really are. When we experience the same thoughts from our Heart, they appear "actual size," and it is easier to have a perspective on how important and meaningful they are.

When a thought has an obsessive quality, charged emotions or deeper layers of conditioning are probably being triggered. And, of course, in the case of seeing a person you are attracted to, this can trigger sexual desire. Such emotions or desires can be explored in the same way as the thoughts: How do you know you are attracted? What is it like to just feel your desire without trying to get rid of it or satisfy it? What else is present besides the attraction or pull of the desire?

Desire can be a wonderful doorway into Presence if you follow it back to its source instead of following it out to the object of your desire. By following a desire back to its source, you can experience more and more of this natural happiness and the sweetness of love that is present in your Heart. What a relief it is to discover that you don't need to satisfy a desire to get to the satisfaction and joy within your Being.

The Gift Life Is Delivering to Your Door

Q: Is life predetermined, or is my friend who uses manifesting techniques successfully onto something? I deeply know the truth, but I feel caught in the ego's separation. How can this imperfect self help others? I want to have an abiding awakening and live as this truth rather than just have a mental knowing of it. I have recently learned to meet everything directly, and although this sounds like a conceptual tactic, I want to face the truth of my moment-to-moment experience fully.

A: Meeting every moment is all that is really required. Our lives are not so much predetermined (although from a certain perspective it looks that way) as much as they are orchestrated moment to moment by a very wise and loving Presence. It is so good at creating this beautiful life and everything in it that it doesn't need a plan. It just improvises everything.

Everything you experience and everything your friend who believes we create our reality experiences is part of this wonderful improvised creation. We recently met a Harvard researcher who is studying consciousness. He told us that it seems that some people are at a point where manifesting techniques are appropriate for them and work for them, while others not at that point can use the same techniques and make their life worse! And those who have used manifesting techniques successfully for years can find themselves at a point where those techniques no longer work and even backfire and seem to cause their life to fall apart. However, he hadn't found a formula yet that explains when or how a spiritual awakening can happen, as it can arise when your life is working or when it's not working at all.

I invite you to welcome all of your experiences, including when you are able to manifest what you desire and when you aren't. Every experience is an opportunity to discover more of the depth, richness, and mystery of this crazy and yet beautiful life. What a blessing it is whenever you can meet life in this completely open way. And when you can't meet life fully, then the blessing in that moment is found in the depth of suffering that not being able to meet life takes us to. Sometimes the Heart has to break open to reach the deepest core.

The awakening you want so deeply is unfolding here as your entire life, including every experience. The life you are living is how life is happening for you. There is no need to compare yourself to others except to notice what else is possible. But however life turns out for you, every experience is a gift that life is delivering to your door in this moment.

Suffering Is a Patient Teacher

Q: *I understand suffering from the perspective of the soul, as suffering often brings needed change and growth. But I'm confused when suffering doesn't appear to have a purpose, for example, when a good person suffers due to severe illness. How can one explain this to their loved ones? How can the person suffering come to terms or even overcome what he or she is going through?*

A: This is a very challenging question, as it sometimes does seem from our limited perspective that suffering serves no purpose. Obviously, we can't know for sure, as we can't always know now the effect the suffering that someone is experiencing may have in the future. We can get a hint of the answer to why consciousness needs suffering by noticing how much suffering opens our Heart. It seems that even though consciousness is infinite, it still likes to stretch itself by opening even wider. Eventually, we learn that we don't need to suffer in order to open the Heart. Once we learn that suffering is not necessary, we can just go directly to love and the softness of compassion. But until we learn this, life keeps reminding us to open our Heart even wider by showing us the suffering that arises when we don't.

Even when we have surrendered and given our Heart totally to the truth, we still experience the suffering of others, so we are inspired to reach out and show them the same love that has rescued us. The pain itself can be a good hurt, like the good hurt from exercise. In the end, it turns out that the suffering was all just an idea of suffering, and what is really happening is this stretching and unfolding of our infinite Heart. There is no suffering in the depths of love, and there never has been.

It can also help to understand the true cause of suffering. Suffering actually comes from our resistance to our experience. That is what actually hurts. There is only pain or suffering when there is sensation or experience and *also* resistance or struggle. The sensations and experiences by themselves are not painful. The good news is that it is actually possible to not suffer even in the midst of a very difficult experience if we simply stop resisting that experience altogether. The greatest gift you can give another is to help that person see that it isn't necessary to suffer, even when he or she experiences tremendous loss or physical difficulty.

Sometimes the best you can do is to just be there with someone who is suffering without suffering yourself. It doesn't serve others to suffer along with them. Instead, you can be with someone who is suffering and shine love and acceptance. The power of this example is profound, especially if you can hold your Heart wide open even when someone is struggling and angry and all of the rest. Not pulling away or trying to change another person's experience but, instead, staying right there with that person with love and acceptance can be powerfully transformative.

Suffering is not a mistake. Paradoxically, our suffering is what finally teaches us to accept every experience and so become free of suffering. We eventually find a way to be free of suffering because resistance and struggle with life hurts. But it takes a lot of discrimination to finally see that the true cause of suffering is our struggle and resistance to an experience, especially when the problem appears to be in the experience or the intense sensations. Fortunately, suffering is a patient teacher.

The Mother of All Habits

Q: *I have experienced a long lasting struggle to come to terms with my suffering. I want to let go, but how?*

A: Suffering is simply the effort to change, fix, or keep our experience. When we are suffering, our attention, or really our love, is flowing to an idea in our mind about what should be happening instead of what is happening. This is the source of all our discomfort and pain. Sensation by itself is not painful. Only when we think about or tell a story about how we want to change, fix, or keep a sensation does a sensation becomes painful.

However, because there is great momentum to our thinking and storytelling, there is great momentum to our suffering. It is the mother of all habits. So even though suffering is so painful, the tendency to strive to change, fix, or keep our experience can continue to arise in both obvious and subtle ways. This is simply the nature of habits—they tend to continue.

Now here is a dilemma: Anything we do to change our suffering is just more suffering. It is one more attempt to change or fix our experience. The antidote to suffering is to see the underlying truth about suffering. In this way, the end of suffering is similar to the realization of our true nature. They are both a matter of seeing what is true more clearly and completely. They aren't the result of something we do, but the result of something we recognize.

Recognizing something isn't something we really do. It's more like something that happens within us. When you look at a photo in the newspaper and suddenly recognize your friend in the picture, it isn't something you do. You don't decide to recognize the person in the picture and then go about making that happen.

The recognition just happens within you. It's a potential you already have, since you already know what your friend looks like, and that knowledge is simply triggered by the photograph.

So what is it we need to recognize about suffering? We need to recognize that suffering is only a thought! It is just an experience created by an idea or thought. If the thought falls away, there's no longer any suffering. Suffering ends when we see that the source of our suffering is simply the thought that things should be different than they are.

Half of the Truth

Q: *I read where you say, "The good news is that even before you trust this deeper knowing, it has been working perfectly all along. The difference is that when you trust it, when you surrender to it, you don't suffer anymore. When, instead, you pay attention to your ideas about how things should be or how you want things to happen, this innate wisdom still gets you where you need to be, but because you are so busy with your ideas about it, you suffer. The good news is that this innate wisdom is not something you add or something you do or something you need to master but who you are." Does this mean that life is happening by itself through me as it desires, and I can do nothing to create the life I want or block life expressing through me?*

A: The limitation of concepts and thoughts is that whenever we speak or write about something, we are only speaking part of the truth. I would even say that the best anyone has ever done is communicate half of the truth! This is true of everyone, even spiritual teachers. And so the quote you refer to offers some truth, but really only part of the truth. Perhaps the value of it is that it offers a part of the truth that is often overlooked or not even considered by most people.

The deepest truth is that there is an innate wisdom unfolding this life that always gets you where you need to go. It is also true that this innate wisdom moves through you as your desires and, even more importantly, as your deepest drives and motivations. It appears that the Mystery that is unfolding this life loves to play and create so much that it even gives you the power to choose and act as an apparent individual. So the ego, or false identity we form, makes choices and takes life and awareness in directions that sometimes cause problems. The ego wants to create what it wants regardless of what Being wants! There's no mistake in all of this. The mystery loves the unpredictable ego that it has created! There is also a deeper movement in us of our essential selves that moves in harmony with the wisdom of Being and yet is still an apparent individual acting and choosing, only we are moving as essence and in alignment with Being's wishes.

Sometimes we are moved by the ego's desires and, at other times, we are moved by deeper drives coming from our essence. Paradoxically, we can even choose what is already happening. How we choose is not often completely one way or the other. There is quite a dance going on between the ego and essence, which allows Being to create unpredictability and surprise within itself. Maybe that's the only way that something that is already infinite and eternal can create and play—by allowing something new and unpredictable to be created within itself.

Again, there is no final truth in anyone's words. If you are enjoying creating and expressing through your desires, then go for it! You can also rest sometimes and explore what life is like when you surrender your doing or, even more simply, notice that life is unfolding beautifully even when you are just observing it. Surrender is not something we do really; it is more a result of the observation of the bigger truth that everything that happens is already a part of the intelligence of Being at work. This recognition naturally leads to a balancing of our tendency to overdo our doing, which is where our suffering lies.

Q: Does the ego have the power to create what it wants to be, have, and do? Does the ego have the power to block the natural flow of life through me? Or can the ego only create psychological suffering or happiness, but it doesn't have the power to block the flow of life or to create what it wants?

Desire and Suffering

A: The ego has a small degree of power to create what it wants and, at times, to block the flow of life temporarily. However, the ego does have a lot of power to cause us to suffer, although suffering itself is just an experience in thought—a mental state. There is no actual thing called suffering. It only exists as a mental experience. Mental suffering can trigger feelings and physical sensations, but the source of those feelings and sensations is thoughts.

For example, there is probably some furniture in the room where you are right now. You can think about the furniture, but the furniture is also a physical reality. Compare that to imagining a baby elephant in the room where you are right now. You can think about the baby elephant and imagine it in great detail, but the baby elephant is still not really there in the room with you. So suffering is all imagined, like the baby elephant. That is why the ego has so much power to cause us to suffer—because it doesn't take much to imagine something. We only have to exercise our imagination to suffer; we don't have to do anything else.

In the midst of this potential for suffering, there are also the events in your life and the actions you take. The ego has a small degree of power to affect these. And when it does, we often learn much more about how limited the viewpoint of the ego is. Oscar Wilde once wrote that there are two great tragedies in life: One is when we don't get what we want, and the other is when we do. When the ego gets what it wants, we often discover the limitations, problems, and difficulties we hadn't foreseen when we were lost in the perspective of our ego's desire. The ego acts out of a very narrow range of impulses that are focused on its own needs and preferences. When these get satisfied, we discover the limitations of our understanding and foresight. A friend of mine always wanted a house in the country with a big yard. When she finally got one, she spent the entire summer mowing the lawn! Spending all her time riding a lawn mower wasn't in her ego's picture of the joy of having a place in the country, and it also wasn't her deepest desire.

So the ego can create distractions and detours that interfere with the unfolding of our life's purpose, but fortunately the underlying wisdom and discrimination of our Being is still also working. So we eventually feel a truer impulse and adjust course and end up back in the flow. Or our ego's creations fall apart and then essence, or Being, picks up the pieces and puts us back on track. Our life is a dance between all these forces. Ego has some capacity to affect what happens, but that capacity is much less than the capacity of our Being to unfold life in truer directions.

When the Heart Tastes Emptiness, It Is Very Full

Q: *Desire is gone, and I move through the days almost like a robot, with no agenda and lacking much action. Foods and activities come and go in an instant. I never know what I'll be doing next. Passion is dormant. It's hard to like anyone especially and hard to decide what to eat or buy, yet it's easy to take whatever or hang out with whomever. I'm alone and enjoying it, and I don't miss relationship, but I do miss someone around to talk and do things with. Any pointers?*

A: What you describe is very common when desire falls away. There can be a kind of dry emptiness when the usual sources of passion no longer move you. Sometimes this happens after an opening or awakening; however, the dryness suggests that there's still a habit of living in the mind. There's nothing wrong with this, but when emptiness is tasted by the mind, it is very empty.

One suggestion is to drop into the Heart and experience the emptiness from there. This can bring back a sense of moistness and even passion without returning to the egoic types of desire and passion. When emptiness is tasted by the Heart, emptiness is experienced as very full.

As for the question of relationships, I suggest dropping into the Heart and simply relating to whatever is present right now. You can be filled with love by loving the floor, the furniture, the sounds in the room, and anything else that is present, including, of course, other people. It is the mind's habit to look around and see that there is no one to talk to. The mind is conditioned to notice what appears to be lacking. In contrast, the Heart notices the endless possibilities for relationship. You can even fall in love with empty space! And if no one else is around, why not talk to your true love? Why not talk to the emptiness itself?

Is the Sky Really Blue?

I shared with some friends some information about the Croatian healer Braco, who helps many people by simply gazing silently at a large audience. I mentioned that I was going to Hawaii to see him, and I received the following question in reply:

Q: I'm wondering if any brief interaction with someone such as Braco is as useful as the permanent, deep healing that comes from an honest and consistent inquiry into one's own true nature. Braco, after all, is not possessed of anything his devotees do not also possess, nor does he claim it. But looking at the faces in the video of him, it is clear to me that those who come to him are seeking healing outside of themselves in Braco's gaze. Seeking is hell is it not? I am curious, is there something you feel you might gain from gazing with Braco? Are you not already at peace? I very strongly felt you were at peace when I met you.

A: I don't see what Braco does as contradictory to inquiry, and it can even be complementary. Let me share the experience of a friend. He had a severe infection leading to a month long coma when he was a young boy fifty years ago, and he has been severely disabled ever since. He recently started gazing with Braco both online and on DVD. He has noticed a dramatic improvement in his breathing, his energy, and most dramatically in his ability to swallow. It used to take him 3-5 minutes to swallow each bite of food. Now it takes him 1-2 seconds. I used to only be able to understand him 10% of the time, and now his voice is so much stronger that I understand him 75% of the time. Interestingly, he is also a lifelong spiritual seeker and has found that it is much easier for him to drop into his Heart since he started seeing Braco. If anything, all of these results will make it easier for him to inquire and contact his inner source of Presence. This is what I mean by the truths being complementary.

My own sense and experience is that there are many levels to the truth, including the deepest truths of pure Presence and Being as well as the practical levels of living in this world. I've had a number of health problems, which Braco has helped me with. In addition to physical healings, Braco evokes a sense of peace and contact with Presence in those who are in his audience. Even though I'm already very much at peace in this life, there is always room for more! I'm open to help or inspiration wherever I find it. Inside and outside are all one thing, so it doesn't matter if I recognize peace within myself or peace in another. Braco is my own Self in a different disguise.

I'm curious where you draw the line? Would you also find it contradictory with a practice of inquiry to seek help from a doctor or dentist? That is also seeking outside yourself for healing. How about hiring a therapist, plumber, or electrician? Would you never call the fire department or the police for help? And is it really *never* appropriate to seek understanding and inspiration from a spiritual teacher or mentor? I'm being a bit extreme to make a point, and I doubt you hold any such extreme views. Even though seeking and looking outside yourself may be limiting and is often a place of suffering, holding some idea that there's nothing you can find outside yourself could be just as limiting.

As I explore and live in deeper and deeper levels of essence and Being, I find that my sense of what is spiritual gets bigger and bigger and includes more and more. Braco is quite a mysterious phenomenon, and I look forward to finding out what possibilities may come from my contact with him that I haven't yet imagined.

Q: *Thanks for your thorough response to my question. I didn't ask it from an attitude of being sure of myself, but rather to possibly dissolve my own possible ignorance. In that vein, I continue with a few questions/observations:*

If what's happening is that Braco somehow transmits something to others through his gazing as opposed to others being the instruments of their own healing via the faith that they bring to Braco, then the Braco gazing phenomena is a justification for seeking, is it not? Rather than seeing that all is divine, characterized by equality of vision, always a gathering of equals, those gathered around are reinforced with the idea that the guru/gazer is something special and has something to give them. If we are one, what can be given?

Some of the sages on a radio program I offer have said that the satisfying of a desire is not what brings pleasure. What brings pleasure is the underlying happiness shining through because of the temporary absence of neediness. I would submit that Braco's gazing is akin to satisfying a desire—to be healed—and that underlying happiness and wellness shine through for a period of time. However, without the seeing through of the illusion of the separate self, the one so healed is likely to need another fix and yet another, which is the hell of seeking. I have a lot invested in the absolute equality of all beings and also in the realization of oneness as the ultimate medicine. Tell me where I may be off here. I would appreciate it.

A: I enjoy this kind of conversation, and I also hold everything lightly and enjoy watching my own perspective shift, grow, and evolve. And especially since I'm probably one of the folks on your show who said that satisfying desires is not the true source of happiness, let me just say that I agree with everything you say.

What I would add is the possibility that all there is, is truth. So since that is all there is, every perspective has some truth or has a contextual truth. And yet no perspective contains the whole truth. Even the idea "The sky is blue" is incomplete. Today the sky is grey here, and at night the sky is black. There can also be different levels of truth that are simultaneously true. From where I stand, the sky today is grey. Up above the clouds, the sky is simultaneously blue. And even higher up, above the atmosphere, the sky is black even during the day. All three statements are true at the same time.

So what you say about seeking being a place of suffering is true, and often it is the most relevant truth. However, it is also true that for some of the people in Braco's audience, that's not the most relevant truth or not their truth. At a certain "altitude" someone could be there seeking physical healing and not really suffer from the experience at all, especially if it works for them. It may be, as you point out, a temporary experience of satisfaction, but it still isn't an experience of suffering. At another altitude (or maybe depth), the whole phenomenon of Braco could be a place of intense suffering, as someone might be wanting so much and either not getting it at all or just getting enough to fuel their addiction to seeking. At still another level, the seeking (and any suffering it entails) is just where they need to be, and the impulse to seek is coming from their essence. At certain points in our unfoldment we need to seek in order go beyond seeking.

And, of course, there is a place where it is all fine and there is no suffering because there's a clear seeing of the bigger truth that everything that matters is found in Presence itself. From that perspective, one can enjoy the experience of being with Braco and also enjoy it just as much when sitting at home alone. As you point out, at that level, we are all equally endowed with this Grace and Presence, and there is nothing to get from Braco and also no problem with getting something from him. As you also point out, at this level there is only one Being, and everyone else, including Braco, is seen as our equal and even as our own Self.

These different levels of the experience are all "true" and are all happening simultaneously within any particular audience and can even happen simultaneously in the same person. We can walk and chew gum at the same time, and we can hold more than one perspective at the same time.

Just for fun, we can also explore the meaning or truth of this idea called suffering or even "hell." Within any experience that we call suffering, there are also levels of truth. Suffering experienced from the inside is a kind of hell, and yet ultimately, there is no actual thing called suffering. It is just a thought or concept we are believing. If suffering were a thing, we would all just have it surgically removed! At the same time that we are thinking that we are suffering, our essence, or Being, is deeply enjoying the experience. The simplest way to cure your suffering is to notice that you are also enjoying your experience and therefore not really suffering that much.

One kind of freedom is to avoid suffering and/or avoid seeking. That provides a certain degree of freedom, and when you are successful, there is no suffering. However, it is still a limited freedom, as it depends on your avoiding seeking. Yet seeking is a natural capacity of the movement of thought, and no one loses the ability to seek and even to suffer. So the freedom that depends on not seeking is still a limited freedom, and there is still a subtle effort (or you could say seeking) in avoiding seeking and even in just holding the idea that I need to not seek. I was struck by how you say you have "a lot invested in the absolute equality of all beings and also in the realization of oneness as the ultimate medicine." That investment could be a subtle form of this efforting and suffering for an idea, even if it is an idea about the end of suffering!

An even bigger freedom is when you have fully experienced the nature of seeking and suffering and found out that there is nothing wrong with either of them. They are both just movements of thought, and there is no lasting harm done by either of them. At the deepest level, our Being enjoys everything immensely, including thoughts and desires. Then you can spend all morning seeking, all afternoon purely inquiring, and all evening resting as awareness, and it's all great! That is a very big freedom, and that freedom doesn't depend on what you do or don't do or even on what you want or don't want. I had a teacher years ago who shared that since he discovered the true source of happiness within, he wants ten times as much stuff as before. Since his happiness doesn't depend on any of it, he just wants it all!

The difference between the sky being grey or blue or black can be a very slight difference in perspective. You can drive up a mountain and all of a sudden come out of the clouds and into the sunshine. There are also endless degrees or shades of any experience. Where does the sky stop being blue and start being black when you are going up in a rocket? Similarly, the distinction between suffering and freedom can be very slight and/or very gradual. Sometimes with the slightest adjustment to our view, the suffering just falls away and is seen to have just been an experience triggered by a thought. Sometimes there is a capacity to hold onto shades of suffering and enjoy the tension between the depth of our essence and the illusion of our ego. I think maybe it was Ramakrishna who used to say that he always held back from the final merging with his Beloved because he enjoyed the longing for her so much.

This bigger freedom isn't something you can achieve. It is ever present as a characteristic of your true nature as Being. In fact, our Being is too damn free sometimes, because it is even free to suffer! But of course, it is also free to let go of suffering and just enjoy the sky, whatever color it is right now.

Rejection and Desire vs. Love: A Talk by Nirmala

An mp3 recording of a talk given in satsang is available to purchasers of this book at:

http://endless-satsang.com/part4mp3

Chapter 5

REALITY AND BELIEFS

Everything is real! Everything that exists, everything that happens, and everything we experience is real. Even illusions are real illusions. An illusion is something real that appears to be something other than what it really is. The smoke and mirrors used by magicians are real smoke and real mirrors! Our minds create images or thoughts that we take to be more real than they are. The thought or mind activity is real, but the content of our thoughts becomes an illusion if we take it to be more than just a thought. We can be tricked by our own minds into believing our thoughts are more real than they are, just as we can be tricked by a magician into believing an illusion is more real than it actually is.

Yet some things are more real than others, and some things are very real and not illusory at all. How do we distinguish how real an experience is? One approach is to notice how long it lasts. In the spiritual tradition of Advaita, the ultimate reality is that which doesn't come and go, that which is always here. Other than the mysterious source of all experiences, nothing else we can experience has this quality, and yet this mysterious source always remains a mystery. The source of experience and awareness is beyond awareness. The source of everything is the ultimate reality, and that is realized, not by experiencing it, but by realizing that that is who you really are. It is realized by being it.

We can use the same criteria on more ordinary things to find out how relatively real something is. The longer something lasts, the more reality it has: A mountain is more real than a thought because a mountain lasts longer than a thought. Because our thoughts and beliefs have some reality when we are experiencing them, we often take them to be more real than they actually are. How long do your thoughts last? Are they as real as a mountain, or only as real as a momentary breeze? The mountain is still here the next day, but is that same breeze? There's nothing wrong with a small reality, with something that only lasts a moment. A beautiful sunset only lasts a short while, but that doesn't make it any less beautiful.

However, it can be useful to discover and distinguish how real our experiences are. It is obviously hopeless to become attached to a particular sunset. Trying to hang on to a sunset only gets in the way of enjoying and appreciating it. The same is true of our thoughts, which last even less time than a sunset. Thoughts are like flowers that bloom and wilt in a matter of seconds, yet we often take our thoughts to be more real than they are. And if a thought has turned into a belief, it's especially easy to treat it as more important than it is.

Beliefs are just habitual thoughts—thoughts we think over and over again. Our parents teach us what to believe by repeatedly telling us what to believe and then we learn to think these thoughts repeatedly ourselves. We come to believe some thoughts so strongly that we assume they are true without even having to think them consciously. Take, for example, the belief, "I am the body": Most people are taught to believe that they are their body. Although it may be hard to recall a time when you didn't believe this, your family had to teach you this. Now the idea that you are the body is assumed in almost every thought you have. When you think, "I'm hungry" or "I'm going to take a nap" and many other daily thoughts, the belief, "I am this body" is implied and assumed to be true.

How much reality does the belief that you are the body actually have? Is the body always here? Is it here when you are deeply asleep? Was it here before you were born? Will it still be here when you die? Do you sometimes completely forget about your body, like when you are lost in a good novel? There's nothing wrong with this belief or any other belief, but is a particular belief more like a mountain or more like a breeze?

The important thing is to determine for yourself how real your beliefs and experiences are. The way to not be fooled by illusions or small realities, such as thoughts and beliefs, is to see their true nature. If something comes and goes quickly or often, then it's helpful to realize that it can't be very real.

Even more important is to notice what is more real than the illusions of your mind. What is here that doesn't come and go? What is here most of the time? The things that are here most of the time are simply more real than the things that come and go.

We have already explored some of the things that are more real, such as awareness and space. A lot of things are more real than our thoughts. The essential qualities of our Being, such as peace, joy, and love, are more real than our thoughts. When we experience these qualities, they are undeniably familiar. Often when people experience their own essence, they are surprised to discover that essence has always been here. For instance, when you experience essential peace, you realize that it has always been here. These deeper realities are more subtle yet more permanent than the outer realities of our lives, which come and go, so we often don't notice or experience these deeper realities. It is only when we touch them directly that we recognize how very real they are.

What is real right now for you? What are you experiencing? How real is it? Is it something that comes and goes quickly, or is it always here? How do you know what is real? There's nothing wrong with something that isn't very real or that doesn't last; that is just its nature. You can simply enjoy it while it is here. And yet, what a profound gift it is to recognize a deeper reality that doesn't come and go. What a relief it is to discover that peace, joy, love, wisdom, awareness, and infinite space are real beyond measure.

Is The Brain the Source of Consciousness?

Q: Am I not just the brain? Is the brain not the source of consciousness and awareness? If not, how can we know this? But if we are the brain, then we are mortal, we will die, and we are not an Eternal Self. Is the experience of awareness simply another state of brain activity?

A: These are very thoughtful questions, and yet they are based on a faulty assumption that is also at the core of most scientific reasoning. Once that faulty assumption is accepted, the logic that proceeds from it is faulty. It's like leaving on a trip and believing you are starting in Kansas when you really are in Montana. When the initial assumption is so mistaken, there's little chance you will arrive at your intended destination even if your navigation skills are very good.

The mistaken assumption is the idea that things are separate. If things are separate from one another, then your questions about the brain are very relevant. The brain is a truly amazing expression of this thing called awareness, or consciousness. So it is natural we've come to assume that the brain is the source of the consciousness that we observe operating through the brain and, really, through the whole body, since the nervous and endocrine systems actually use the entire organism to think and perceive. But what if this assumption of separateness is mistaken? What would that mean about the body/brain organism and its functioning if it isn't separate from anything else? What if there is really just one thing here? Then what would be the source of the awareness?

Just as scientists can no longer think about the brain and its functioning as separate from the body because thoughts are actually happening in the entire body, we can't accurately consider thought as something that happens in one body. Every movement of consciousness that we recognize as thought or awareness is happening in the entire field of awareness that our bodies and brains appear in.

I read recently about an experiment based on the unique brain wave patterns one observes when a bright light is directed into just one eye. Scientists chose two complete strangers and introduced them to each other for a short conversation, then separated them into two rooms that were electrically shielded from each other. Scientists found that if they directed a bright light into one person's eye, the person in the other room would exhibit the same brain wave activity as the one whose eye was being illuminated.

While this seems impossible if we believe that the brain is a separate object, existing apart from all other objects, this result becomes quite possible (although no less amazing) if we assume that the two brains in this experiment are part of one thing called consciousness and if this miracle we call awareness is actually arising in the space, or field, where the two brains are both appearing.

The idea that objects (including brains) are separate and unconnected explains much of what we observe, but it doesn't explain the results of that experiment or many other aspects of our experience, including insights, intuitions, psychic abilities, and mystical experiences.

In contrast, the idea that one consciousness is expressing through every brain and every thing doesn't contradict any of our experiences, including those that seem to suggest that we are separate beings. For example, your left hand can be scratching your ear while your right hand is writing a letter without contradicting the underlying reality that your hands are both part of one being. And so, your brain can be discussing something with or even arguing with my brain, even if we are ultimately one thing.

So the idea that everything is one thing fits with and explains more of our experience than the idea that we are separate entities. This suggests that the idea that everything is one is a truer idea than the idea that everything is separate.

Who Is There to Do Something?

Life is going to unfold however it unfolds, and there isn't a lot we can do about it. Still, we can do a little to affect how it unfolds, and that is also part of the unfolding. So when I suggest you check what is true, it is to affect this little bit that we can do and that we can choose.

Q: Who could do this? It seems our view of this affects everything. So who is this "you" that you are referring to? It seems the I is only a thought.

A: This question about doership is a very fundamental one. But humor me for a minute: Before you read any further, reach up and touch the top of your head. The *you* that can determine what's true and isn't very true, and the you that can make choices and take action is the same you that just tapped the top of your head.

The bigger truth is that life will unfold according to the will of the divine. If you leave out this truth, you will suffer from thinking life is all up to you, which is a setup for either a sense of failure or false pride. However, if you leave out the smaller truth that you still need to choose and act, you will suffer from thinking there is nothing you can do. If this incomplete view is taken all of the way to its logical conclusion, then there is no one to ever do anything, and you might as well just stay where you are right now and starve to death. But even then, you haven't escaped the smaller truth, since you will find that you have to choose to keep sitting there, even as you get hungrier and hungrier.

The balanced view is to leave everything up to God, except what's right in front of you to do in this moment. If you are hungry, eat. If you are tired, sleep. If you are sick, find a way to heal. If there is a choice to be made, check what is truest to do and then do it. Then you can forget about the results of your actions because that part isn't up to you. That part is up to the bigger truth of God's will. There's a line in the *Tao Te Ching* that goes something like this: "Do your work and then step back." This points to the truth that our actions are up to us, but the results of our actions are not.

What Do I Do When There Is No Doer?

The following is from the free ebook That Is That *by Nirmala, which is available at http://endless-satsang.com/free*

Spiritual teachings suggest that there is no doer, that there is no separate self that is the source of our actions. This teaching often causes a lot of confusion, as it is contrary to our experience. It seems that there is a doer and that *I* am the doer: *I* get up in the morning, *I* walk the dog, and *I* drive to work. How do these things happen if there is no doer? And if there is no doer, then what do I do? How do I live my life if there is no one here to live it? What do I do if there is no doer?

This confusion exists because spiritual teachings point to something that doesn't exist in the usual way. The nature of reality can't be described or explained with words, and it can't be experienced through the ordinary senses. In speaking about something that can't be spoken about, the easiest approach is often to use negation. If you can't speak directly about something, then you're left with saying what it is not.

So spiritual teachings contain a lot of negation: There is no self. There is no doer. The world is an illusion. Not this. Not that. Negation can be effective in pointing us away from illusions, such as the idea of *me*, and other false and mistaken ideas. If you take a moment to look for yourself, you discover that there is no individual self, only an idea of a self. The "I" is just an idea. So in this sense, it is accurate to say that there is no self and no doer.

However, the mind can't conceive of or even really experience nothing. If you are experiencing something, then that is by definition not nothing. So when the mind is pointed to nothing or to the absence of a self or a doer, it makes a picture or concept of nothing and thinks about that. If we are told there is no doer, the mind makes a picture of the absence of somebody, something like an empty chair or a broom sweeping by itself.

Again, this contradicts our actual experience: There is something in the chair when I sit down in it. The broom only sweeps when I pick it up and start sweeping. So there is obviously a distortion or inaccuracy in the approach of negation. While negation does evoke a certain experience of emptiness that can be spacious and restful, it doesn't capture the totality of reality. It leaves out our actual experience of the real world.

Another approach is the opposite: Instead of saying there is no self, there is no world, and there is no doer, we can say there is only Self, the world is all one thing, and it is this totality of existence that does everything. In other words, *everything* sweeps the floor and sits in the chair. If we look deeply into our experience, we can see that there is some truth to this perspective. If we trace back all of the causes of any action, we see that there are an infinite number of influences or causes for the simplest action.

For example, you may sweep the floor because your mother taught you to keep a spotless house and your dad taught you to be responsible, not to mention all the other messages you received from the culture and society about cleanliness and responsibility. Add to that all the people that influenced your mom and dad and everyone else who ever had an impact on you. And what about all the factors that led to the particular path of evolution that gave you those opposable thumbs that allow you to use a broom? If you include all the factors at play when you pick up a broom and sweep, you can see how it might make sense to say that everyone and everything is sweeping the floor. There is a doer, but it isn't you; it is everything. And by the way, all of these factors are at work if you don't sweep the floor. Not doing something is just another thing we do.

This approach of including more and more instead of negating everything is also a useful teaching tool. It evokes a sense of the oneness and richness of life. But again, it doesn't capture the actual experience of an action like sweeping. If only *everything* would sweep my floor, then *I* could go take a nap. Speaking about everything as the doer of everything that is done also doesn't capture the sense of no self that is experienced when we look within using spiritual practices such as self-inquiry.

So if it isn't complete to say that there is no doer, and if it isn't complete to say that everything is the doer, what's wrong with just saying that *I* sweep the floor, and be done with it? For purely practical purposes, saying "I" do something is enough. But as already noted, saying "I" leaves out the many rich and complex causes of our actions, and it leaves out the absence of a separate self that we discover when we look within. It also doesn't suggest that there's more to this reality than meets the eye.

So we are left with a dilemma: It's incomplete to say that there is no doer, it's incomplete to say that everything is the doer, and it's incomplete to say that I am the doer. It's like a multiple choice test where all of the answers are wrong! Yet, what is it like to not have an answer? What's it like to hold the question even when you've exhausted all of the possible answers?

The question of what is going on here, what is this experience of doing, can be a rich experience in and of itself. Such a question can put us more in touch with our experience than any answer can. The question invites a direct sensing of the various levels of our experience. As the broom moves across the floor, is it possible to simultaneously experience the emptiness within, the richness of the oneness of all things, and the personal actions of our particular body? Why do we have to choose one?

And what about the original question, "What do I do?" Could this also be a rich opportunity to explore all the dimensions of existence? Why does there have to be a right answer? Can the question, itself, evoke a deeper sensing of life and an endless willingness to question again and again? What do I do now? And what about now? The gift may be in the question itself, not in some final answer. Life is unfolding in ever new and different ways, so maybe only in each new moment can we discover what the *everything and nothing* that we are is going to do next.

There is an assumption that spiritual teachings are supposed to bring us spiritual answers, that we are supposed to finally get somewhere. But what if the point of this spiritual journey is the journey itself? What if the answers are true and relevant when they arise, but they become irrelevant in the next breath? So perhaps the question of what to do isn't meant to ever be done with or fully answered. Letting go of the idea of a right or final answer can make the question come alive in this very moment. What are you doing right now? What is most true to do now? And then, what about now? It's always time to ask again because it's always a new now.

Just for this moment, find out what happens if you just allow yourself to not know what the right thing to do is, who would do it, and even if there is anything to do, or if doing even really happens. When you question that deeply, is there more or less of a compulsion to act in unhealthy or ignorant ways? Or is there a natural curiosity and sense of wonder that arises and puts you very much in touch with all of the mysterious elements that make up this particular moment? Does this curiosity lead you to rash and silly decisions, or does it allow impulses and intuitions to arise from a deeper place within your being? If you know less and less about doing, what happens next?

The gift of the deepest spiritual questions arises in the day-to-day living of life. Asking, "What do I do?" can lead you on an exploration that has no boundaries, and the journey can only start here and now. What most often limits us is our conclusions. The simple antidote is to ask another question: "What do I do when there is no doer, when everything is the doer, and when it's also up to me to do something?"

What Happens When We Die?

Q: If I feel oneness, will I still feel that sense of oneness after my death? Do Buddha, Ramana, or Jesus still feel the oneness as they would have felt it when they were alive?

A: This is a good question, although no one can really answer it until they die. There are some mysteries that are meant to be mysteries. When it comes to something like death, what we don't know will always be more than what we do know. Not knowing something can actually be very rich and exciting.

So far, based on my experience with living, my guess is that there is no formula for what happens when we die. Just as everyone's experience of life is unique, it seems likely that everyone's experience of death would also be unique. Some people might dissolve back into the oneness without any trace of individuality remaining. Others might have an expanded sense of their true nature but with a sense of identity as someone who is experiencing the vastness of Being. And others might retain a strong sense of individual existence, which might suggest that they would reincarnate again to satisfy their remaining karma or individual desires.

We all eventually get to find out what happens when we die. In the meantime, we have the mystery of what is going to happen before we die! Will I fall in love today? Will I be happy or sad today? Will I realize my true nature today? There are endless small mysteries to be discovered every day and even some big mysteries. Your question is a good one because it shows curiosity. Since life and death are so unpredictable and unknowable, your curiosity can serve you much better than any answer to your questions. It can be very surprising to discover that questions are almost always more satisfying than answers.

Q: *You mentioned "many lives." If you don't actually know what happens when we die, then where does the theory of many lives come from?*

A: As for what happens when we die, I hold all perspectives lightly. The biggest truth is that I don't know for sure what happens when we die. That being said, within that big mystery of not-knowing, are many possible perspectives about what happens when we die. My own sense is that all perspectives have some truth to them, including reincarnation. However, no perspective contains all of the truth. Reincarnation raises as many questions as it answers: Who or what reincarnates? Where are we in between reincarnations? Can you "remember" future lives as well as past lives?

Holding perspectives lightly can even allow you to not know and to know something at the same time. You don't need to hold onto either knowing or not-knowing. And you don't need to limit yourself to one way of knowing versus another. Why limit yourself to one perspective or another? Why take a permanent position about anything, including the fixed position of "I don't know"? Life doesn't seem to limit itself to the ideas and beliefs we have, and it also doesn't limit itself to the known or to the unknown. It dances in and out of all of these experiences.

I hope this helps make it clearer why I sometimes contradict myself. Putting anything into words immediately limits and distorts the actual truth. Sometimes in order to speak more of the truth, you have to contradict what you just said. If you can hold all of it lightly, then you can benefit from all of it without being trapped by any words or beliefs. Words don't contain the truth, they just point to it.

No One Has Ever Spoken the Whole Truth

Q: I read confusing and contradictory teachings about our true nature and what complete realization is like, and yet sometimes I can just follow the simplicity of choosing to allow and letting love be my guide.

A: Before enlightenment and after, everything is complete and also always becoming. That is just the nature of consciousness. The different levels of our being all exist, but they are not all as real as the level of our true nature. A single drop of water is still wet, but it isn't as wet as the ocean. All the levels exist as a way for oneness to experience itself a little at a time, which isn't better or worse than an experience of the totality, but it does provide a variety of different experiences. In fact, there is no experience of the totality, as at that level, there is nothing separate to experience itself. So the totality needs all of the levels and illusions to have any experience at all!

The teaching of every teacher is still partial and often so is their understanding. It's possible to move beyond normal perception, but when someone comes back into the body to speak about that experience, the description of it is somewhat diluted and distorted by putting it into words.

My suggestion is to hold everyone's teachings lightly, including mine and your own thoughts and conclusions. You don't need to reject them or ignore them, as they all do have a piece of the puzzle. But no one has ever spoken the whole truth, and I would suggest no one has ever really had a grasp of the whole truth. So their words always include some limited understanding.

It's okay that you don't have a hold of the whole truth, because the whole truth has a hold of you! Your own experience, including the love you are cultivating and allowing, is your truest teacher. This mystery of existence is revealing itself to you in every moment and is choosing to do so in a unique and exquisite way. Every person's discovery of their true nature is different and unique by design. Why repeat any experience when there are so many ways to reveal the infinite truth?

This true teacher inside you speaks through your Heart in the language of love. You are right that the mind can, in a sense, choose to allow and choose to love. When it does, a bigger love moves more fully through you. So the mind chooses, but it is the Heart, or true nature, that actually loves. This is putting the mind in service to the Heart instead of having the mind be in charge all the time. The mind is like a private that thinks it is a general. So I invite you to explore all the complex and contradictory teachings and understandings and then to return to the simplicity of your own Heart. Why leave either one out?

Now You See the Ego, and Now You Don't

Q: *The teacher in my Heart led me to "turn from the mind of me," and it was a four-fold process. When I turned from pride, I was totally humble. When I turned from greed, I felt contentment for the first time in my life. When I turned from desire, I was filled to overflowing with gratefulness. And when I turned from fear, I finally found my Heart as a place I could go to rest. Maybe because I had lived such a stressful, fear-filled life, this place blew me away. I turn every morning to my Heart, and it is so wonderful that I started asking how to live from this place, how to stay. It wasn't long before I found your book* Living from the Heart *among some books I had bought but put away. I had to laugh at the speed of this answer. Anyway, I loved your book and have a question that maybe you could clarify.*

I can totally understand awareness being so small and constricted in the mind and being so full and expansive in the Heart. But I don't fully understand your explanation of the me—that the me in the mind is still awareness but just limited. I always thought Hindu belief was that the me is the ego, an illusion. In fact, when I am turned to the Heart, I am not aware of me. There is no me. All I feel is healed and whole, not separate like the me in the mind. Is the me awareness, or is it just another thought of the mind?

A: I would always point you back to your own experience first. When you don't experience the me or the ego, it is either gone or so small as to be completely unnoticed, like the tiny dust motes floating in the air in front of you right now. The dust motes may exist and be real, but you may not be experiencing them at all. And even if you are, they are only of the most passing interest because there's so much more here that is more substantially real.

It may just be a matter of semantics, but I like to speak about the ego as being included in awareness because I find that allows an open curiosity about the ego and the *me*. If they are around and kicking, it can be helpful to explore their nature as fully as possible. One thing you may quickly discover is that the ego and the *me* have a very short existence, even shorter than those little bugs that are born and die within a few hours. The ego and the *me* only exist when you are thinking about them, and they only exist as thoughts, which is a very limited existence. Since thoughts come and go so quickly, it is more accurate to speak of the hundreds or even thousands of egos that we experience in a single day.

As you mentioned, some Hindus say that everything that comes and goes is illusion and only that which never comes and goes is real. I tend to use this definition in a more gradual and relative way, with shades of gray instead of just black and white ideas of real and unreal. I suggest that you can tell how real something is by how long it lasts, so there are many things that are much more real than thoughts. However, in this way of defining what is real, thoughts are still real but just barely so, and even when thoughts are not happening, we still have the potential to think them again. So something that is even more real than the thoughts that make up the ego is the capacity within awareness to identify. In this view, the ego is a trick that awareness can play—now you see it, and now you don't!

I point to the reality of thoughts, the mind, and the ego to inspire a full discovery of their nature and to acknowledge that if everything is oneness and Being, then nothing is left out, no matter how insubstantial, short-lived, or illusory.

Another way to see the many thoughts and patterns of identification that make up the ego is as a necessary developmental stage. It's easier to go beyond identification with the ego when you have developed a healthy, functional ego. The ego may be extremely limited, especially when compared to our essential true nature, but that doesn't mean the ego never has a function or never serves us in some way. The capacity to identify may be part of what develops through the experience of the ego. Perhaps the ultimate freedom is a completely flexible ability to identify and dis-identify in each moment, as is called for in the moment.

In any case, an important thing to notice about egoic thoughts is how narrow awareness becomes when we think such thoughts. Contracted is the correct way for awareness to feel in those moments, as that is how awareness itself discriminates how small such thoughts are and how little reality they have. When we are experiencing a *me*, it is appropriate for awareness to feel contracted and tight because that identification isn't very real or true. Discovering that a limiting thought is not very real can be as liberating as discovering that a profoundly big and real truth is true. In both cases, you have put the experience into perspective and seen how real and how important it is.

What matters most is your own experience. You don't need to discriminate the nature of the *me* or the ego when they are not here! Then you can just enjoy the more limitless and spontaneous flow of awareness that naturally occurs when identification with thoughts isn't occurring. You can trust the contraction that happens when an egoic thought arises, and you can trust the expanded sense of being that happens when you drop into your Heart and there are no thoughts.

The Spectrum of Being and Doing

The tradition I come from is a path of knowledge, so this path often uses a lot of words. This path uses the mind to go beyond the mind, but the point is what lies beyond the mind. What is beyond the mind isn't separate from or lacking in the mind; it just also extends beyond the mind.

So I invite you to approach the words I use in a particular way because they aren't really the point. It is possible to approach the words very gently and hold them lightly, especially the content of the words. Just let the words carry you somewhere and don't worry too much about what's being said or try hard to "get it" or even remember any of it. Treat the words like you would a good story. Remember story time when you were a kid? What a relief it was when it was story time because you didn't have to remember anything, and there wouldn't be a quiz about it later. You could just sit back and let the story carry you, let the words have whatever effect they had on you without worrying about holding onto what was being said.

The path of knowledge is a path that is meant to take you beyond knowledge and beyond words. And yet, I want to speak to you about a very specific word, which is *Advaita*. It's the name of the tradition I come from. It's a Sanskrit word that means "not two." What that word is pointing to, what that word is meant to carry you to, is the experience of oneness. There are not two things. There's only one, one existence, one thing in this whole world, in this whole universe. It's all one thing.

When people hear about the experience of oneness, they often think, "I wish I could have that experience. Show me the way to oneness," as if it's only found somewhere else, as if oneness is somewhere other than right here. So I'd like to take a look at oneness and explore what it means if there's only one thing.

There's a funny thing about the dualities in the world, all of the ways we create contrast, differences, and even opposites: If you look, you discover that dualities are really just one thing in different amounts. There is only one thing that you can experience more or less of.

For example, we talk about light and dark as if they were two different things, or even opposite things. But light and dark are really only one thing, and that one thing is light. Light exists, but dark does not. Photons make up this energy we call light, but there's no such thing as "darkons." Darkness doesn't exist as a separate form of energy. "Dark" is just a word we use when there is less light. It's just a way of describing the experience of not much of the one thing that does exist, which is light. Light exists everywhere in the universe—even the darkest place has some photons or cosmic rays zipping through it.

Another example is hot and cold. Hot and cold sound like two different things, but they are really just one thing: heat. Hot and cold are just different amounts of heat. Like light, heat exists everywhere in the universe, but when there's not much heat, we call that cold.

Another example is deep and shallow. They are different amounts of just one thing: depth. If there's a lot of it, we call that deep; if there's not much of it, we call that shallow. So whether something is called deep or shallow, it depends—it's relative to something else. For example, we might consider water deep when it is over our head. But if you're a giraffe, water that is over our heads would still be shallow.

With deep and shallow and other dualities, there is no clear boundary between these apparent opposites. Because we're talking about different amounts of one thing, there isn't a clear cut place where deep becomes shallow, dark turns to light, or cold becomes hot. These designations are relative. If you live in Canada, 79° Fahrenheit is hot. If you live in Arizona, where I'm from, 79° is kind of cool.

This starts to give you a flavor of the oneness we are speaking about when we speak about Advaita. We're not just talking about some big experience, some *thing* you can only taste during a spiritual experience. Instead, all experiences are different degrees of this oneness. It is through the apparent dualities of light and dark, hot and cold, and one versus many that oneness creates contrast and differences. It's actually how oneness creates all of experience.

What does this mean about you, about the oneness of you? We can explore this by looking at another kind of apparent duality, and that's the duality of being and doing. If you explore this as a duality, you'll find that being and doing, although they are very different experiences, are actually just different amounts of the one thing that exists, which is being—which is also what you are.

There are moments where you're very far into the experience of doing and that experience has very little sense of being to it. Those are moments when doing is coming from a shallow place of being we call the ego. When doing comes from the ego, it tends to involve a lot of effort and activity. This kind of doing is about making something happen, getting something, or going somewhere so that someday you can just rest and be.

There are other moments when doing has less efforting and more of a sense of fullness that comes from being. Examples are things you do, not for some purpose, but for their own sake, like dancing, skiing, or reading a good novel. When you do such things, there's more of the sense of beingness to it. There is more of a sense of fullness that is already full of what matters, already full of all the qualities of being, with more peace and joy and love.

Other times, there is such a fullness of being that doing becomes totally irrelevant. Everything is already complete, and doing no longer computes. Any doing would be superfluous and unnecessary. When there is a very complete experience of pure being, there is little or no need to fix or change anything. As a result, there can be very little or no activity, and yet the experience is complete and satisfying.

So there's a spectrum of being and doing. But doing and being are really just one thing: being. Doing is just being in action, being expressing just a part of its infinite capacity. That's how this world of appearance gets created—when being does something. Being becomes less by doing; it experiences less of itself. Anytime you do something, by definition you are not doing or experiencing everything else. Everything you can do is always here in your being as a potential action, and yet you can only do one thing at a time.

The point of looking at being and oneness this way is to help give you the sense that this one Being is already here right now. Yet when we hear about being and doing, we often ask, "How do I experience more being?" We hear about being and turn it into a prescription for more doing—doing something to get to more being. Unfortunately, trying to experience more being takes us more into an experience of doing! Trying to get expanded, contracts us!

Another possibility is to just be curious. What is your experience like right now? If everything is being, then it doesn't matter whether your experience right now has a "doing" quality to it, which gives a direction to being, an objective to it, or if being is more at rest as pure potential. In seeing that your experience is just different amounts of one thing, you might find oneness right here, right now, in whatever is happening or not happening, in whatever you're doing or not doing. Oneness just is. It is in every moment, in every experience, and in every thought. Thought is just a doing; it's just an expression of being. Oneness is in every feeling; feeling is just a particular kind of doing, a particular movement or expression of being. Everything is made of 100% being.

If you explore this apparent duality of being and doing, you'll find that you can never find a doer. All you ever find is doing. What seem like doers—the identities, the forms your sense of self takes on—are another doing. Identification, or a sense of *me*, is another activity, or doing, that happens. So whether you're washing the dishes, clipping your toenails, driving across town, listening to someone talk, or lost in thought, whatever you have conceived of as the doer of those things, turns out to be another doing. The doer is another thought, another activity, or motion in your mind, another motion within this one field of being.

The idea that there's only doing and no doer can bring you back to here and now. What's really going on here? What does it mean if there isn't a doer, just a lot of doings? Even experiencing is a doing. There is no experiencer, just a doing of experiencing. And the oneness is not really an object of experience—it's what you are. Once you catch the flavor, the taste of this oneness, it doesn't matter anymore what you experience, because all experience is just your *being* doing something. Experience is never bad, it's never wrong, and experience is always changing. But if everything is oneness, then it doesn't matter what you experience. What matters is what you are. What matters is the oneness.

And you already are what you are! No extra doing is required to be what you are. Doing doesn't ever separate you from oneness. You can do and do and do, and what you are remains the same. Doing happens, but doing is not that important. Doing is just a play, a wonderful expression of what you are, but being what you are doesn't depend on doing or not doing.

The experience of what you are is different when doing stops. When doing stops, there's more of an experience of what you are. But that doesn't mean Being is absent if you happen to be doing something. If you happen to be wiggling your fingers, adjusting your posture, or scratching your nose, being doesn't go away. So the question isn't how to stop doing or how to do the right thing or how to do less. The question is: "What is oneness like right now? What is being like right here?" Wherever it is or whatever being is doing, that's cool! It's amazing that being can do so many things. Where is all this doing coming from? What is it that remembers to breathe when you're asleep? What does that? What is a thought? Where did it come from? Who *does* thinking? There you are minding your own business, then all of a sudden words pop into your head! Where did they come from? Who did that? You can't find the doer. Anything you conclude about the doer is just what you conclude. The conclusion is another doing. It's just another thought!

So what's your being/doing like right now? How deep, how shallow, how light, how dark is it, how empty, how full, how busy and how complete is it—not how do I get more or less, but what is it like right now?

Slaying the Dragons of Our Core Beliefs

Q: *I've been inquiring into beliefs. Is it helpful to uncover the core beliefs that are the source of more superficial thoughts and ideas and then to do inquiry to address those core beliefs?*

It's like there is a big forest on fire. There are five or six dragons standing in the middle of the forest. They light the forest on fire by breathing out fire everywhere. If we put the fire out, the dragons will start the forest burning again. But if we kill the dragons, the fire will stop. The fire is the outer layers of conditioning, and the dragons are the core beliefs, or the inner layers. Would you keep your main attention on the core beliefs, or give the same amount of attention to everything?

A: You are definitely correct that core beliefs are often the source of our more superficial thoughts. Practically speaking, it is helpful to address these core beliefs with inquiry, as you've been doing. I would also suggest that you don't have to actually kill the dragons, as they are, after all, just made of thoughts. Instead, I invite you to become very curious about your thoughts: How do you know what you think? How do you know that something is a belief and not just an idle thought? How do you sometimes know what you "unconsciously" believe? What are thoughts and beliefs made of? How important are they really? If they are just thought dragons, maybe you can turn them into pets!

Underneath the dragons are even more fundamental beliefs that we often aren't aware of and don't stop to question because they seem so obviously and undeniably true. These are core assumptions, such as, "I am a person" or "I am this body." One very deep assumption is the idea that some experiences are better than others. When you combine this belief with the belief that you are a separate somebody, then it seems true to work hard to get a better experience for this separate me. But if you see that no experience is any better than any other (they are just different), or that there is only one awareness that is having all experiences, you can hold this whole journey of life lightly, including all the endless ways you can inquire and question.

Since no experience is better than any other, the point of the inquiry is not to get rid of or get more of anything, but simply to discover what is happening. In the case of your deepest assumptions about life, you can be curious about the beliefs that it doesn't even enter your mind to question. How do I hold a deep belief or assumption so that it doesn't seem possible for it to not be true? And in the exploration of all of your beliefs, you can ask not only what you believe, but also what the nature of belief itself is. And what is the nature of the awareness that experiences even the deepest beliefs? Does awareness need to be changed or fixed in any way?

The Game of Believing

Q: When I'm alone, just resting as awareness, my mind can feel so free, relaxing in not-knowing. Let's say I've spent four days like this, and then I'm with my friend. We talk and I become sucked back into knowing, and my mind feels more rigid. The conversations we have are always about what is not true. He believes something, but I don't. For example: We're driving in a car, and my friend says, "Oh, my God, imagine if we just crashed there. That would be so horrible!" What do you say to something like that when you don't believe it? And yet, because I still fear rejection, I might say, "Yeah, that would be gruesome!" Then I feel I was sucked back into that kind of knowing. I'm wondering what spiritual teachers talk about. Nothing you can talk about seems to be true. What do you talk about with your wife and friends when you don't believe things?

A: The way I talk with my wife or friends hasn't changed except that there is greater ease with everything, including just sitting in silence. This means I'm willing and able to talk about anything, including the deepest spiritual stuff and also petty, personal stuff or even silly, ridiculous stuff. Whatever happens is fine with me. Even being bored by what is being talked about is fine with me. Boredom is not fatal!

Every moment is a wonderful opportunity to see how our being responds and how our ego responds. What a gift it is that you can spend time alone and drop so deeply into not-knowing and resting. And what a gift it is that your friends can still catch you up in believing something with their words. As you understand more and more about how this all works, you may find that you can be with your friends and continue to rest in not knowing, even as you are having a normal conversation.

The key is this thing we call believing or identifying. What is that? How do you believe or not believe? What's different? How do you know you believe something? You can say something you don't believe and know that you don't believe it as you are saying it, so just saying something is not the same as believing it. And yet when we or someone else says something, there's a natural pull to believe it also. Our awareness loves to fully experience thoughts and ideas, so awareness does this weird thing—it becomes those thoughts, or becomes identified with them. So we say we believe this or that. Identification is like dressing up for Halloween and forgetting we are wearing a costume. We hold the belief—which is just a costume—to be real. Isn't it amazing how we can see something happening but not actually experience it because we don't believe it? Or how we can believe something so strongly that we see it, feel it, and experience it even though it isn't actually here?

Believing is not black or white. When you and your friend are talking about having an accident, you can believe it a little and experience some of the fear and drama of an accident, or you can believe it a lot and have a full-blown panic attack. Or you can hardly believe it, and the thought passes through your awareness without making a ripple.

Belief is one of the ways we interact with the world. It is not a mistake, and being takes great pleasure in all the different degrees to which we believe our thoughts. However, as your awareness of this game evolves, you may naturally be less and less interested in beliefs. Just as you have little or no interest in the games you played as a child, you may find yourself less and less interested in your beliefs or in believing anything. You don't need to play the game of believing to live your life, and you also don't need to give it up completely. It can be fun to go to a movie for a couple of hours and believe what you are seeing, although even that can get old.

After all, there is a big and real and mysterious world of experience here that is not dependent on your believing anything. Why watch a movie of life when life is right here in front of you? Why watch a belief in your mind about life when real life is happening right now?

"Why?" and "Why Not?" Cancel Each Other Out

Q: I was searching for truth and peace for quite a long time, but at a certain point I felt there was nothing to search for as everything is just happening of itself. I was the one who was searching, the search itself, and the nothingness that was found, all at the same time. Life is just what is. The question is: What meaning does spiritual teaching and pointing to the obvious have in all of this, if everything is just happening spontaneously? Everything has become so easy and simple, and yet there are so many teachers, gurus, and words making it complicated.

A: First, I will answer your question very simply, and then I will use your question to, as you say, make it more complicated. I receive many forms of the question you have asked, where someone wonders something like, "If everything is unfolding as it should, then why would I go to work, try to understand anything, save the world, etc.?" Sometimes the question is in the form of "Why not?" For example, "If everything is always perfect, then why not just sit on the couch all day, why not quit my job, or even why not jump off a cliff?"

The best answer to any of these questions is the opposite question. Why offer spiritual teaching? Why not offer spiritual teaching? Why not sit on the couch all day? Why sit on the couch all day? The biggest perspective on life doesn't hold onto making anything special, but it also doesn't hold onto any resistance to anything. If everything is unfolding just as it should, why would that not include spiritual teachings and spiritual teachers and even words that make things more complicated? It is in the willingness to ask both sides of the question that things can become simple again. Of course, it is fine if you never go to another spiritual gathering or read another spiritual book. But it is also fine if you or anyone else does do these things. And while it may ultimately be ok if someone chooses to sit on a couch for the rest of their life, there is almost never a good reason to do so!

When we discover the truth that everything is already fine just the way it is, sometimes our ego latches onto this truth and uses it to question something we don't agree with or find useful anymore. There's nothing wrong with this, and I have yet to meet someone who doesn't sometimes use this bigger truth in this way. But when we are willing to ask the question in both directions (e.g. Why have spiritual teachings? And why not have spiritual teachings?), then there is a recognition of space around all possibilities and room for all kinds of spiritual and non-spiritual expressions. And, of course, this means there's room for you to enjoy the simplicity you have found, which appears to have little need for spiritual teachers.

So that's the simple answer: Why not? Or if the original question is, "Why not?" the simple answer is, "Why?" Since there is no reason why and no reason why not, these two questions cancel each other out and leave lots of room for everything else. If you just want to hear the simple answer, you can just stop reading here.

However, seeing that from the biggest perspective it doesn't matter what we do or don't do doesn't change the fact that we still have to decide whether to do something or not. There are several levels to truth, and while the biggest truth is that it doesn't matter what we do, from a practical level it may matter whether we go to spiritual gatherings like satsang or not, whether we go to work or not, or whether we brush our teeth or not!

These different levels aren't separate and are all part of one thing, so they do affect each other. And although they are not separate, they are different. So the truth that operates on one level is not necessarily the most important truth on another level. On the level of the Absolute—from the biggest perspective—nothing really exists and so nothing really matters. On the relative level of our existence, everything exists and everything matters. On this level, we get to create or choose the beliefs and values we will live by. If you want to be comfortable and well-fed, then valuing work and practical matters will serve you. If you want to be spontaneous and live simply, those values may not matter very much to you. If you want to deeply understand and explore the truth, then spiritual teachings may be of interest to you. If you want to live without subtle spiritual distinctions cluttering up your awareness, then words may not matter as much.

Contact with the biggest truth of the inherent perfection of everything tends to dissolve any rigidity in our values and beliefs. If ultimately it all doesn't matter, then what I choose to make matter on the relative level matters less. The ego creates the rigidity in our belief structures that we developed to sort and handle our relative experience. As we experience more and more of the ultimate perfection of everything, the rigidity of these egoic structures begins to dissolve. Contact with our true nature naturally allows us to hold our beliefs more lightly.

The dissolving of our egoic structures can bring the dilemma of what to do to a new, deeper level of questioning. If we don't hold any rigid views about what is right or wrong, how do we decide what to do? What guides us? At this point, many swing back and forth between hiding out in the Absolute perspective that what we do doesn't matter or returning to some old, rigid egoic view of what matters. There is another possibility. There is another level of our Being, and that is our essence.

Essence is the deeper, purer, subtler expression of our Being that includes such qualities as love, compassion, wisdom, clarity, joy, and peace. Ultimately even these don't matter, but on the more relative level, they matter much more than the daily concerns of life, including the practical question of what to do. When we are in contact with our essence and these wonderful qualities of our true nature, we are able to make choices based on wisdom, clarity, and loving kindness. This contact results in more ease, growth, evolution, beauty, freedom, love, and peace in our life.

When the question is about how to live from essence, spiritual guidance and teaching can serve. This is because spiritual teaching, at its best, demonstrates the flexibility to move between the different levels of reality and can evoke that same flexibility in others. Ideally, spiritual teachings also serve to help put you in touch with your own essence and inner guidance. Although it isn't necessary to have a spiritual teacher to develop more contact with essence, a spiritual teacher can be helpful. Ultimately, there is no reason to live from essence, and yet our essence exists and is here to help guide and unfold our life. Why live from essence? Well, why not live from this deeper place within you? Why not experience all the limitless peace, joy, and love available within you? If a spiritual teacher or teachings helps you do so at this point in your unfolding, why not use them?

What Is Real? A Talk by Nirmala

An mp3 recording of a talk given in satsang is available to purchasers of this book at:

http://endless-satsang.com/part5mp3

Chapter 6

Daily Life

How does spirituality relate to daily life and to the psychological and practical dimensions of our human life? Is spirituality separate from and unrelated to these concerns, or is our true nature interwoven with our minds, our bodies, and our world?

There is just one reality that makes up this world and everything that lies beyond this world. The deeper dimensions of our Being are different than the physical and psychological experiences that make up ordinary life, but they aren't separate. Since everything belongs to the oneness, everything affects everything else: Everything that happens in your daily life will have some effect on your realization and contact with essence, and every movement of essence or realization of your deeper nature will have some effect on your daily life. Understanding this is relevant to understanding spiritual awakening and how spiritual awakening affects and is integrated into daily life.

Typically after a spiritual awakening, we experience a kind of honeymoon period, where the thoughts and behaviors that make up our ego are either gone or so lightly held that they don't matter. However, this period usually doesn't last, and sooner or later the old identity reappears. Many have experienced something similar after coming home from a spiritual retreat: Once they are back home with their family and in their old job and routine, the old reactive patterns return, and eventually the old identity reforms. Although we are never completely the same after an awakening, at some point we often re-identify with the old separate sense of a self to some degree.

Some spiritual teachings focus on seeing the illusory nature of our usual identity. This can be a powerful approach to dissolving the false identity of the ego and can catapult someone into an experience of no self. However, without a balanced perspective that also addresses the conditioning and beliefs that support the ego's existence, the realization of no self is often followed by either a return to the old identity or spiritual bypassing, where an identity has reformed based on the new concept of no self. This idea of or identity as no-self is then used to avoid admitting or addressing the remaining conditioning of the ego.

Other spiritual teachings or practices focus on the gradual dissolving or purification of our egoic conditioning so that when a deeper realization occurs, the ego identity is less likely to reform. However, this approach has its own trap of becoming an endless journey to an imagined spiritual destination that is never reached. There is no end to what could be understood or dissolved because life is always creating new challenges and even new conditioning. Processing our psychological conditioning is not a goal in and of itself. The point of spiritual work is to help us hold the spacious experience of a profound realization without our old patterns and identifications reforming.

What we do and how we live our lives matters, not just because of the benefits of having our act together, but because healthy physical and mental functioning create the comfort and balance in our life that make it possible to integrate the spiritual realizations that Grace bestows on us. So having a balanced and effective means of caring for, housing, clothing, and feeding ourselves matters. Having some degree of psychological understanding and growth matters so that we can function and relate to the world and others in a mature and healthy manner. However, ultimately we do these things, not to be a better person or build up our spiritual ego, but in service and devotion to the bigger truths that can be revealed to us and expressed through us.

As your realization deepens to include not only the emptiness of existence, but also the deeper dimensions of essence that are the divine at play in the world of form, your human nature and daily life can become another arena for the realization and expression of your true nature. Your true nature loves to create, dance, and play within the physical and mental dimensions. Full spiritual awakening includes finding out how your deeper nature functions and responds to the very human challenges we all face in daily life. There is just one thing that is living your life and everyone else's too. What an opportunity our daily life is to discover the truth about the nature of this alive mystery that is creating it all!

Pulled in Two Directions

Q: I feel quite torn between fully living my life, including all of the ordinary human activities, and devoting myself completely to enlightenment and the deepest truth.

A: I would simply suggest that it doesn't have to be one or the other. Give 100% to life sometimes and give 100% to enlightenment sometimes. That will allow you to experience both of these aspects of life fully. Eventually, you will find they aren't separate. But as long as you do experience these aspects of your life as separate, then just alternate between moments of giving yourself totally to the juicy, alive experience of being ordinary and human and moments of giving yourself totally to the experience of not knowing and possibly not even existing as a separate being. There is no contradiction, so you don't need to stop yourself from doing one or the other.

When you feel torn between these two aspects of life, that is an opportunity to notice the confusion or the feeling of being pulled in two directions and to give yourself 100% to that. It is in giving 100% to our experience that we can see the whole truth of it. The antidote to any difficulty is to experience it fully. You don't need to figure out ahead of time what the right thing to experience is.

It is in this willingness to experience the many dimensions of your experience and existence that you become able to distinguish and understand the entire range of your experiences. You don't have to get rid of anything, but you can find out more about everything.

Tell the Superego to Shut Up

Q: I had a glimpse of the truth, but the bliss and general happiness isn't here now. I had a very painful past and am still running that story, even though I understand that beneath psychological pain is a story created by my thoughts, and I'm not my thoughts. The story is made of some strong social "shoulds," and I have a strong inferiority complex. I hope you can show me some direction as to what to do about it.

A: I invite you to become very curious about your experience when these thoughts are arising. How do you know what you are thinking? Do they appear as pictures, voices, feelings, or sensations? If you take each of these one at a time, are they bad experiences? Is a picture in your mind a bad experience? Is a voice a bad experience? Or are they just particular experiences?

Especially, explore your feelings and sensations. How do you know you are feeling inferior? What are the sensations in your body? Are they bad sensations or just particular sensations? You may discover that the images, thoughts, feelings, and sensations are not a problem, but just particular experiences with no real meaning or significance. Allowing the images, thoughts, feelings, and sensations and becoming curious about them can be a very rich exploration. After all, they aren't really yours; they are just side effects of reactions and beliefs you inherited from your family and society.

It's not up to you how often these reactions and responses show up or for how long. But you can choose to give the images, thoughts, feelings, and sensations a lot of love when they do show up. I'm not suggesting that you will enjoy them or like them, but you can give them the essence of love, which is acceptance and attention. By letting your thoughts and reactions be here and by being very curious about them, you are giving them what they always wanted, which is love.

There is one exception that might seem contradictory to what I just said. When you're experiencing an internal voice, image, or felt sense of someone criticizing or attacking you, then defend yourself from the attack. Tell the voice, which is the voice of the superego, to shut up or leave you alone, and mean it! Keep defending yourself until the voice or attack stops. Paradoxically, defending yourself against the superego like this is actually a way of embracing the energy of it. Please note that I'm not suggesting telling other people to shut up or go away, only the internal voices and images that criticize and undermine you.

When you're experiencing an internal image of someone criticizing you, you have projected your own strength and power onto that idea of an authority. By defending yourself and turning the tables on the inner image, you reclaim the energy of the strength and power. Then from a place that is full of energy and essence, you can explore and allow your own experience, as I suggested earlier, and decide what is true and what needs to be done or not done.

Negative Feelings Are Doorways to Essence

Q: I sometimes wonder how much I try to push my negative feelings down because I'm on a spiritual path. Do I really have to see feelings like hate and anger as the "bad guys?" These feelings keep reoccurring, no matter how much spiritual work I do. Maybe I should just accept them as they come up and say, "Hi, it's you again."

A: You're right when you suggest it's possible to just accept these negative feelings when they come up. These feelings are totally normal and natural, and if they come up, then they come up. Once you allow them to just be there, it's possible to discover that you don't need to express them or take them out on anyone else. You can just let the feelings be there as strongly and fully as they happen to be.

Something that can help with accepting and allowing these feelings is to let them be bigger than your body. The difficulty with negative feelings is they sometimes seem so huge, especially anger, which by nature is a very expansive energy. When we try to hold such feelings inside our body, the pressure builds up and the feelings tend to explode out into actions we may later regret. But if you let the energy and feelings be bigger than your body, the pressure won't build up inside of you. If you let the anger fill the entire room or even the entire neighborhood, then all of that red hot energy of anger has plenty of room.

You can take this a step further and explore these feelings more deeply. What is anger like? What sensations are present when you are angry? Are these actually bad sensations or just particular sensations (especially if you let them be bigger than your body)? What's underneath these sensations? What memories arise when you allow the sensations to just be there? Are any other feelings hiding beneath the feeling you are having?

As you allow and explore the feeling, you may find that new insights or understandings come up about that feeling. You may also find, surprisingly, that underneath even the most negative feelings lies a more positive quality of our essence that is driving the outer feeling. Many of our feelings are the ego's attempt to express or control some deeper quality of our essence.

For example, the feeling of anger is an egoic version of true strength, which is a quality of our essence. Our essence is capable of a tremendous strength, capacity, and directness in its discrimination and action. However, when you were growing up, if it was not okay to experience the strength of your essence, you may have developed an egoic version of strength to stay in touch with this aspect of your essence. Some people stay in touch with their essential strength through anger, while others accomplish this by suppressing any anger and appearing weak. By allowing and exploring the anger or the experience of weakness and vulnerability, you may uncover the essential strength underlying these egoic reactions. The key is neither to express nor suppress your experience, but to feel it as fully as possible and explore it as fully as possible.

All of your experiences, including strong feelings, are profound and unique doorways into the deeper truth of your Being. However, the most open doorway to your true nature is the experience you are having right now. In fact, that is the only door to your Being that is ever available to you. Fortunately, life provides you with an endless array of experience to explore and dive into, and in each moment, life brings you the experience you most need to explore and understand. Will you accept the opportunity for exploring your Being that is opening for you right now, even if it appears as a negative feeling?

True freedom isn't when you no longer have any experiences you don't like or don't want (which is an impossible goal). True freedom is when you discover that every experience is a potential opening into the deeper realities of Presence and Being. Then you are free of the need to change or fix your experience and you can, instead, embrace it and discover its endless richness and depth.

Life Is a One-Room Schoolhouse

Q: How do I reconcile the teachings of the Law of Attraction with nondual teachings? I wonder if involvement with the mind by trying to create a different reality would interfere with the deepest recognition of my true nature.

A: My own sense is that there are many levels of truth and that they all exist at the same time. On one level, it is true that you can manifest and create your reality, at least to some extent. However, it is also true, on a deeper level, that divine intelligence is unfolding everything from a bigger perspective. It seems that this deeper truth can override the smaller truth offered in teachings about manifesting, which may be one explanation for why people don't always get what they want when they apply the principles of manifesting.

An even bigger truth is that everything is an illusion (even you!), and it doesn't matter what happens. When we experience this bigger truth, there's a natural relaxation of effort and struggle. Everything is fine no matter what happens.

You asked about reconciling these different levels of truth. I would suggest that there is not a better level, but just different levels of truth. The levels don't contradict each other but complement each other. To me, the ideal is not to experience the biggest truth and somehow stay there, but to have the flexibility to try on different perspectives and to be able to play freely on all the different levels. For this, it isn't necessary to reconcile the different levels of truth, since they are already reconciled. They co-exist quite naturally and easily without any need to change anything about any of them. You can play however you wish with these levels: You could spend your mornings playing with manifesting your desires, your afternoons surrendering to the divine plan, and your evenings penetrating all illusions and dissolving the sense of any separate self who could do anything about anything.

There's no right or wrong way to play in this life. It does seem that this human experience on earth is meant to be a place where people at these different levels interact and to some degree affect each other. In a way, this planet is like a one-room schoolhouse, with some people in daycare, some in kindergarten, some in elementary school, some in high school, and some in college and graduate school—all in the same classroom. In such a classroom, the adults would naturally have more to talk about with the other adults, but they might also enjoy playing with the infants, children, and teenagers and may even find they learn a lot from them. And you can imagine how the younger students would also benefit from contact with the older students.

Within each of us, these different levels interact and exist simultaneously. Your own psyche and soul are also a one-room schoolhouse, where all levels of your being exist simultaneously. There's no right or wrong way of experiencing the multifaceted being that you are, just different ways.

To fully experience your pure nature as awake, empty space, it's true that the mind needs to be relatively silent. However, that doesn't make the moments when the mind is active and the illusion is capturing your attention wrong or bad. Furthermore, the distinction between various levels isn't black or white, as there are many levels in between dissolving into the source of existence and full identification with the body and mind. Why not find out about all of these levels, especially since it's not really up to you when the mind falls silent or not? That isn't something you do, but more like something that happens to you. What you *can* do is be very curious about all the different levels and experiences you have each and every day. Experiencing every level fully and with deep curiosity naturally allows more ease in shifting and dissolving the boundaries and attachments that can keep you from moving more flexibly between the levels.

Ultimately, however, every experience is already an expression of an even bigger flexibility. Consciousness even seems to also love getting stuck in various experiences, at least for a while. But then it always gets unstuck sooner or later. It is so flexible that it even allows itself to get stuck! So what I'm offering isn't really a prescription for how to become more flexible in your awareness, but a description of how amazingly flexible your awareness has always been. By being curious about the endlessly different experiences that show up, you may simply recognize more and more deeply how beautiful and mysterious your existence is and always has been. This can lead to not only a realization of the deepest truth of your nature, but also a fuller realization of the infinite capacities and dimensions within it.

Motivation After Spiritual Awakening

Q: *In 2009, my personal story was seen through, and it dropped away. With it, went all motivation. Without a self, there's no desire or fear of living or dying, and without those desires and fears, there seems to be no drive. I have about two months of money left in the bank and no desire to get a real job. Still, I have no worries and sleep like a baby. It feels wonderful, appreciative, in-touch, pure, loving, and connected. The lack of motivation seems to be the biggest part of the "problem." The other part of the problem is a lack of identity. Not having an identity to pin myself to is disconcerting. What motivates you when there is no "you?"*

A: Although there is no formula for what happens after awakening, I can assure you that your experience is not unusual. I have two suggestions. The first is an invitation to become very curious about what is present in the lack of motivation. Because the deeper movements or drives of essence are quieter and subtler than our old egoic desires and attachments, it can take a very sensitive ear to hear them. It sounds like you are already in touch with them when you say, "It feels wonderful, appreciative, in-touch, pure, loving, and connected." So what is that appreciative love flowing most naturally and authentically to? Where do you still find a deeper longing in your Heart? Since every expression of the mystery is unique, even every snowflake, what that deeper longing will look like in your case is unpredictable. Being in the flow of your essence may mean continuing to rest and be quiet, or it may mean becoming busier than ever. The key is to be very curious about what is true in your own Heart. What allows the deepest opening of your Heart right now? I know of a man in California who had a profound realization and then sat on his couch for months. One day, he suddenly had an idea for a spiritual bookstore. He said he was too lazy to *not* get up off the couch and start working sixteen hours a day to open this bookstore. At that point, it took more effort to sit still!

The second thing I would suggest, which may seem to contradict my first suggestion, is that you consider not waiting for motivation to show up. I had a teacher once who pointed out that the word "energy" comes from words meaning "into the work." He suggested that energy and motivation often come once we are already doing something. So you might simply notice what opportunities or activities naturally present themselves and just do them. That will give you a chance to find out if there is motivation or energy for that activity after all.

I see these two suggestions as complementary, not contradictory. The truth is subtle and has many levels, so sometimes we need to sense the subtle movements of our Being, and other times we need to just get up and do whatever presents itself to do. I find that, as the discovery of the complete range of my true nature continues, I experience a greater and greater range of movements and motivations. I'm willing to experience everything from a deep sense of resting (what one of my teachers called "the contented old cow state") to a passionate flurry of activity and creativity. Our true nature includes all of these possibilities and more.

As for the issue of a lack of identity, I have two similar suggestions. One is to be curious about what is present in the space where there is no identity or sense of self. "Beyond No Self," which is included as Appendix 1 of this book, is an article I wrote that explores this further. Reading this may help you become more accustomed to the lack of a self, which is such a strange and unfamiliar experience when it first arises. Once you discover all the rich dimensions of Self that are present in the absence of an egoic sense of self, you might not find the absence of that egoic identity to be a problem.

The second suggestion is to allow yourself to have whatever identity is needed in any moment. Put on an identity when you need it or feel like it, in the same way you might dress up for Halloween. Freedom is when you can spontaneously identify or dis-identify based on what's true in that moment. Spiritual teachings often emphasize dis-identification because so many people are stuck in identification. But there's no reason to, then, get stuck in dis-identification. You can play within the limitless range of roles, stories, and dramas that life contains without getting permanently stuck in any of them.

Guilt Is Not Very Useful Nor Meaningful

Q: I have a problem with guilt. Can you offer any perspectives on guilt?

A: I suggest you notice the contraction you probably feel when you feel guilty. This contraction is telling you that it isn't very true that you are guilty. The truth is what opens your Heart and your sense of Being, so when something causes a contraction, that means it isn't very true.

Although there may be a little bit of truth to the experience of guilt, guilt is not usually a very useful or meaningful concept. And it especially doesn't lead to useful or meaningful action, which is one reason that guilt is not very true or important. Surprisingly, guilt doesn't even often lead to changing or correcting the behavior we feel guilty about. In fact, we often act less kindly and compassionately when we are feeling guilty because of the overall discomfort we feel when we feel guilty. This suggests a more practical definition of truth as that which is useful or leads to a desired outcome. If something doesn't lead to a desired outcome, then it isn't wrong or bad; it just isn't very true.

When you feel contracted because of guilt, just let that contraction be there and get curious about what else is true. If you've done something that triggers a sense of guilt, then there's a lot more to discover about that experience besides how guilty it makes you feel. What else is true about your actions? What were your intentions? How have you been conditioned to act in that situation? What other effects did your action have besides the ones you feel guilty about? Are you even sure that you hurt or harmed someone? What else did you do in the situation besides the actions you feel guilty about? What else do you feel besides guilty? What can you do now that will affect the situation? Is there something you can apologize for or do to make up for your unkindness to someone? How important is this experience in the overall context of your life? And finally, what else is going on in your life besides this particular situation? Guilt may be present, but a lot more is happening than that!

There are endless questions that can uncover more and more truth. Why settle for a not very useful or meaningful conclusion that you are guilty?

The Ego Is a Pimp

Q: After destroying one's ego how do we transact in this world? Can you please clear this up?

A: The ego has always been just a thought, so it has never really done anything. I sometimes say the ego is like a pimp: It stands around and takes a lot of credit for doing nothing. Something else called Being is living your life. Being is very good at living your life, whether egoic thoughts arise or not.

Being creates your experiences through the filter of the egoic thoughts when they are present, since Being itself has no preference for what happens or what it experiences. This filtering of Being's actions makes it appear that the ego is doing something, since the ego's thoughts are having an effect. But the creative force that is actually acting is still Being.

Once the egoic thoughts are dissolved or even just loosened, the same creative process generates lots of experiences and actions without those actions being filtered through the ego's beliefs. Being has always been beating your heart, growing your hair, and getting you up in the morning and off to work or whatever you do. It can and will continue to breathe and work and play and love and all of the rest once the ego is out of the way.

Leaving or Staying When You Get Contracted

Q: *When there's a contraction around a person or situation, how do you know when it's time to move away, without trying to change the person or situation, or when looking at your own aversions, judgments, or self-sabotage is called for instead?*

A: The truth is whatever opens your Heart or expands your sense of self. In contrast, something less true will cause a sense of contraction. If we expand this definition a bit, the truth is whatever opens the most Hearts of the people involved for the greatest amount of time. Not just your Heart, but the Hearts of everyone involved are responding to any unfolding situation or interaction.

So in response to your question, staying in a situation and examining your aversions and judgments makes sense when that leads to a bigger experience of truth within yourself and within those involved. On the other hand, if staying in a situation causes you or others to contract even more, then leaving that situation makes more sense. To effectively question your own reactions and aversions, you may first have to leave a situation. If you are already contracted, then any inquiry you do while you are in that situation may not go very deep.

You can't know in advance if any inquiry you do will lead to an expansion of awareness or not. You just have to try doing some exploration and inquiry within yourself or with the other person and see how it goes. The good news is that there's no harm done if you end up more contracted, because awareness isn't harmed by contraction. If contraction continues, you can leave the situation and do the inquiry in a more conducive setting. I hope it goes without saying that if a situation is dangerous or abusive, first protect yourself or leave the situation and then do any inquiry in a safer setting.

More generally, whenever two people interact, there are two possibilities. One is that both people are equally contracted or equally expanded. This is a comfortable and stable situation, making it easy for both people to be around each other. The other possibility is that one person is more expanded than the other. When this occurs, the more contracted person tends to feel a kind of discomfort, while the more expanded person is usually okay with the difference. This discomfort often causes the contracted person to try to get the expanded person to contract by criticizing, teasing, confronting, or possibly even by being overly complimentary. These are generally unconscious reactions to the discomfort the contracted person is feeling in the presence of someone who is more expanded.

When you are in a more expanded state than someone else you're with, it doesn't serve anyone for you to become more contracted. The effect of your expanded awareness can be an opportunity for a less expanded person to expand. If you find you can easily stay expanded, and some expansion in the other person is happening or seems likely to happen, then it might be true to stay in the interaction. However, if there's little or no chance that the person who is contracted and trying to get you to contract (consciously or unconsciously) is going to expand, little can be gained from staying in the interaction and risking that you will also end up contracted.

Defending vs. Acceptance

Q: How does acceptance apply when you can make a decision to act against something that could harm you? For example, if a person tries to attack me with a knife, should I accept or love this attack and not defend myself against it? After thinking this through, I think maybe I should accept it, meaning not argue internally against it, but also fight or defend against it and then accept whatever the result may be. I would love to hear your thoughts on this.

A: Your question highlights the fact that there are different levels of truth, and your conclusion is a good one. On the practical human level, you need to respond to an attack in some way, which may include defending yourself. On a more subtle and yet more profound level, you can also accept the whole experience.

These levels are not separate and they do affect each other. After an inner attitude of acceptance becomes more established in you, you may respond to an attack differently than you would have before. Instead of fighting back, you might turn the other cheek (especially if no knife is involved!) or simply run away or even find a way to connect with your attacker so that he or she no longer feels moved to attack you. This inner acceptance and equanimity allows for a wider range of responses.

I'd like to add that acceptance isn't actually something you do but an inherent quality of what you are. You are empty, aware space, and nothing is more accepting than space. So practicing acceptance is kind of like practicing having shoulders. Just as practicing having shoulders doesn't make you have shoulders, so practicing acceptance doesn't make acceptance happen. It just allows you to be more aware of the enormous amount of acceptance that is always here. This acceptance, which belongs to your Being, even accepts all your resistance and judgment.

Often the easiest way to notice and experience the acceptance that Being has for everything is to first notice that even when you are rejecting something about your experience, you are also accepting your thoughts about rejecting it. Being, or space, allows everything you like and everything you don't like, and it also allows all of your liking and not liking.

Q: *How do you respond if you happen to see someone molesting someone else? Is it okay to just let someone harm others? It seems that if we were enlightened, we would perceive everything as one, so we would just let someone harm others without attachment.*

A: This is a common question because it's confusing to the mind when two opposite things are both true. So while it is true that everything is one and there's nothing that can harm consciousness, it's also true that you can act without attachment in a situation such as the one you described.

Here's a simple metaphor to illustrate how two opposite things can be true: On a rainy day, you experience thick clouds and some rain. And yet, above the clouds, the bigger truth is that the sun is still shining. I call it a "bigger truth" because the sun shines on the entire earth, not just on the clouds above your head, and the sun shining is more constant and longer lasting than a rainstorm. However, just because it's true that the sun is still shining (behind the clouds) during a rainstorm doesn't mean you go out in your bathing suit and some sunscreen to work on your tan! Your experience of clouds and rain is still real, so you may want to wear a raincoat instead.

When it comes to the hurt and violence in this world, the bigger truth is that consciousness is not harmed by the pain and suffering. Yet while this is true, the pain is still real, and it still may be possible to do something to prevent or stop the violent or hurtful act or at least to help soothe or heal a person who's already suffered from such harm.

Knowing the bigger truth, that there is no lasting harm, can free you to respond to whatever is happening. There's nothing to lose, so why not help someone if you can? The value of this bigger perspective is that it can allow you to see the hurt and violence but not be traumatized or overwhelmed by it. When we don't see the bigger truth, our reaction to the pain in the world is often to avoid or deny it because the pain can seem too horrible to acknowledge. Seeing the bigger truth allows us to better respond to pain and is also likely to make us more willing to respond.

Realizing that love and peace are still present even in such situations—that they are always here "behind the clouds"—unlocks our capacity to be compassionate toward the victims of violence and even toward the perpetrators. This may allow us to stop someone from being violent in a loving and compassionate way. In contrast, responding to violence with more violence usually just breeds more violence.

When it rains, it's not the end of the world. The sun is still shining and will eventually come out from behind the clouds. You don't need to overreact to the rain, while you still might take appropriate actions to stay dry. And even if you do get wet, it's often not that big a deal.

Letting Sexual Energy Be Bigger Than Your Body

Q: Sexual desires are interfering with my work and disrupting my connection with my spouse. How do I deal with my strong sexual desires?

A: Sexual energy is one of the most powerful energies we experience through the body. So if that energy isn't explored and experienced fully, it can be problematic. You might consider some kind of couple's therapy or counseling with your spouse. Often when something isn't working sexually within a relationship, something else also isn't working in the relationship. Although therapy doesn't take the place of spiritual practices, therapy and spiritual practices can support each other. So I also invite you to continue with any spiritual practices you may be doing.

When the sexual energy is strong, something very simple you can do is let the sexual energy be bigger than your body. Trying to hold so much energy within your body can create a pressure that pushes to explode into action—including through orgasm! Letting the energy be bigger than your body relieves that pressure and allows you to feel a lot of sexual energy without necessarily having to act on it. With less pressure inside, exploring the sexual desire itself becomes more possible. You can ask yourself: "How do I know I want sex? What are the actual sensations of desire? Are these bad sensations or just particular sensations?" And when you are being sexual, find out more about that experience by bringing more curiosity and inquiry to that.

Reducing the pressure and exploring your experience in this way can also allow you to question what is true for you regarding your marriage and other sexual relationships. Some important questions you might ask yourself are: "What do I really want? Do I want to leave my marriage? Do I want to damage my marriage? Do I want to find a deeper intimacy within my marriage?"

If you take this question, "What do I really want?" all the way, you may discover what your sexual desire is really about. Often we try to experience more love and connection through our relationships and our sexuality. But what if love is always available, whether or not you are being sexual or in a relationship? Sex might matter a lot less if you were able to experience the love and intimacy that exists in every moment, with or without sex or even with or without a relationship. Then sexuality would become merely an expression of this love and connection with life rather than feeling like sex is the source of connection and satisfaction. (You can read more about this way of connecting and experiencing love in "Love Is for Giving" which is included in this book as Appendix 2.)

Drowning Your Fear in Love

Q: *When I hear people expressing their beliefs, I want to get people to agree with my beliefs or think of me in a certain light. Lately, when I'm approached by someone asserting a strong belief, I see them doing the same thing. Still, an overwhelming desire arises in me to get them to see it my way, but that's just another viewpoint! When I notice I'm doing that I let it go, usually by not responding or by smiling, listening, and allowing them to speak but not taking what they say personally. Not taking it personally is the hardest thing!*

A: Viewpoints are only a problem when they are held rigidly. When we hold our viewpoints lightly, we are more able to recognize that all viewpoints have some truth to them. Then we can share and explore our own and other's viewpoints and be enriched by them all. This doesn't mean all viewpoints are equally true, which is the trap the media falls into when they try to present a "balanced" report and so include a viewpoint that has almost no truth to it. But by holding our own and other's viewpoints lightly and exploring them openly and thoroughly, we can determine how much truth a viewpoint has.

When we hold our viewpoints lightly, we are less likely to feel threatened by other people's viewpoints and therefore less likely to feel a need to change someone else's mind. There's room for all viewpoints. You may also find that introducing someone to your viewpoint is much easier if you first express some agreement with that person's viewpoint.

The reason people hold their viewpoints rigidly is simply because they are afraid. Holding any idea or belief rigidly is a response driven by fear. There are two movements within life. One is love and the other is fear. All movement is motivated by one of these. Love is the movement or expression of our essence. It includes everything from a sweet personal love for a lover or child to a profound sense of the divine oneness and goodness of everything. Love includes all of the qualities of our Being: awareness, spaciousness, aliveness, and connectedness all rolled into one. Love is our essence. It is what we are made of, and it's the most real and true thing there is. In contrast, fear is any movement of thought that restricts, constricts, distorts, or limits the flow of love. Fear is a conceptual structure in our mind that limits or distorts our experience of the limitless love that is always here. Love exists outside of thought, while fear doesn't exist except as a movement of thought.

Like many of the things that seem to be dualities, love and fear are not actually two opposite realities. The apparent duality of love and fear is like the apparent duality of wet and dry: Only one thing exists, and that is water. When there's a lot of it, we call that wet. When there isn't much of it, we call that dry. Dryness is just a concept. Similarly, fear is not an actual thing; it is simply a word we use to describe the relative absence of love. Fear is any movement of our ego or mind that restricts or limits our experience of love and thereby gives us a dry experience that is relatively empty of love. The love is not actually destroyed or gone; it's just not in our experience anymore.

Holding rigidly to a viewpoint or belief is a movement of fear because it limits or constricts the flow of awareness. By this definition, all ideas and beliefs are movements of fear, as they limit or direct our awareness and love. However, this is always a matter of degree, as some movements of thought constrict our experience of love more than others. Furthermore, this capacity to limit or direct awareness isn't bad or wrong, but the mechanism that consciousness came up with to create the entire world and all its experiences and illusions. To experience something, we have to limit or direct awareness. That is how Being creates contrast and differences. To use a metaphor, in a world made up completely of water, without a way to dry things out, everything would always be soaking wet. In this world where the only reality is love, without ideas, beliefs, and even fears, we would be drowning in love with no contrasting dryness.

To further clarify this, there are also two forms of fear. One is objective fear, which is a physiological response to an actual threat or danger in our environment. This type of fear is a healthy part of our organism, as it can protect us. The second type of fear is activated when our mind imagines a threatening or dangerous outcome and triggers the same physiological effects in our body and the same restriction and contraction of our awareness. This type of fear isn't wrong, but it creates all of the drama and misunderstandings of our ego-driven experiences. Most of our mentally-generated fears have *some* truth to them, in that they *can* happen. But most of these fears have very little truth to them, as they don't usually happen.

People disagreeing with us can trigger deeper fears about what will happen if we are wrong or if others continue to believe something that is wrong. If we are afraid, then we will try to get others to change their minds or try to convince them that we are right. But our fears about what will happen if we or others are wrong are not usually very complete or true. What we fear may not happen at all or things might turn out quite differently.

Fear is the driving force behind many beliefs and ideologies. For example, many on the political right are afraid of the concentration of power in the government. Given the path of history, their fear has some truth to it. On the other hand, many on the left are afraid of the concentration of power in corporations and the wealthy, and their fear also has some truth to it. But neither of these fears contains the whole truth, and because of that, the solutions on both sides tend to be one-sided. In this way, fear has the power to reduce our awareness of the truth.

To give fear a chance against the stronger and more powerful reality of love, fear has the advantage of just needing to create the appearance of there being a problem, and often then our mind creates even more thoughts and more fear. Just a thought of something bad happening is enough to trigger fear.

What can we do when a fear seems so real? The simple antidote is to love your fear. Give your thoughts and fears the same fullness of attention and curiosity you would give a new lover. Loving our fear allows us to see it more fully and clearly and to realize how small it is. Fear is a small truth masquerading as a big truth. Loving our fear enables us to see through this disguise. Just as you don't need to get others to change or drop their viewpoints, you don't need to get rid of or go to battle with your fears. Instead, just drown your fears in love!

When someone is sharing their viewpoint and it triggers a fear in you, just love your fear, love your own viewpoint, and love that person's viewpoint, no matter how small it is. It doesn't cost you anything to love this way since the supply of love is endless. In this moister atmosphere of flowing love, the relative truth of all viewpoints can be recognized and enjoyed.

Seeing Love in Every Action

Q: *The quote in your exquisite book,* Living from the Heart, *"But when we see the loving nature of even murder...." needs expansion for me.*

A: When I point to love as the true nature of even a murderous act, I'm not denying the horrible tragedy that murder is. I'm only pointing out that it is love that motivates and animates the murderer, even when that love is so narrow and distorted that the end result is tragic. One quality of love is that it is caring and takes care of that which is loved. Even murderers are trying to take care of themselves or something else that they love, even though the way they go about doing that is limited, misguided, and so ineffective that the end result is terrible.

If we look deeper, we can see that all dualities in this world are really just different amounts of one thing: Light and dark are different amounts of one thing, which is light. Hot and cold are different amounts of the energy called heat. And so it is with love. Love is the energy or force that moves all of life, and yet we can experience such a tiny amount of love that that experience is a dark and cold one, so dark that it can motivate tragically harmful acts even while someone is attempting to take care of themselves.

Seeing love at the heart of every action enables us to respond with compassion and forgiveness even when we may still need to take appropriate action to stop a violent act or prevent it from happening again. So for the victim, family, friends, and even the perpetrator, the ability or willingness to see love at the core of every action makes it possible to not respond to the murderous or violent act with more violence and judgment but with loving compassion and understanding, which may begin the long, difficult process of healing the murderer's pain and suffering and lead to rehabilitation.

Our best protection from violence is to heal the wounds in others and in ourselves that lead to violence, not to treat perpetrators with hatred, judgment, and violence (although we may still need to take appropriate action to protect society by preventing the murderer from doing further harm). It is love and compassion that will lead to a reduction in the violence and horror in this world. So anything that allows us to respond in these painful and difficult moments with more love, clarity, understanding, and kindness is a gift to both ourselves and the world.

Q: You say there is love in every action because love is the nature or essence of everything. Can this lead to a denial of or even justification for cruel and horrible actions?

A: You're right that seeing love in everything can drift into a denial of or justification of unkind or even cruel and horrible actions. However, it is equally a kind of denial to ignore the love that is present in every action. That denial is even more likely to be used to justify further cruelty, shame, violence, and destruction. When we deny that there is love at the core of another person, then it seems justified to punish him or her with further violence and shame.

The antidote is to see the whole truth about a situation: We can see that the essence of all action is a kind of love or caring, and we can also see that this love or caring can become narrow and incompletely experienced and expressed, and sometimes even tragically and horrifically narrow and therefore dangerous and destructive. If we are able to see the love in every action, our own response is more likely to be loving and compassionate. We recognize that hurt, pain, and fear are what are contracting the essence and love so horribly. So instead of inflicting more shame and hurt to punish someone and thereby perpetuate the cycle of shame and violence, we address the shame and hurt in order to possibly heal it and release everyone involved from their suffering.

Just to be clear, this response to the whole truth about the situation includes doing whatever is possible to prevent someone from doing harm in the first place and to protect ourselves and others when necessary. Often this can be accomplished without further violence or shame when we are clear about what the problem really is, and so our actions are in direct response to the hurt, fear, and pain that are fueling the violence instead of being only an expression of our own fear and hurt.

Our mind seeks a world where everything is black or white. But with more experience and maturity, we come to see that the world is the way it is and not the way our mind wants it to be. This real world is incredibly complex and subtle and, at the same time, has an underlying simplicity or oneness of love. Seeing the whole truth and responding to that instead of to our limited ideas and beliefs about good and evil is a tremendous challenge.

Evil is the result of experiencing very little love, which is what happens when we are lost in pain and fear. Realizing this can inspire the experience and expression of more love and compassion, while denying the presence of love in even heinous acts only perpetuates the cycle of violence and hatred. Denying the presence of love in everything is as incomplete a perspective as denying the violence and cruelty in the first place.

So what will you choose? Will you choose to respond to shame, hurt, violence, and hatred with more shame, hurt, violence, and hatred? Or will you make the radical choice to see the whole truth about the hurtful or cruel act and so respond to it with love, compassion, and understanding as well as protective strength, discrimination, and integrity?

Authenticity and Love

Q: I'm no longer able to be inauthentic with my boss to try to get his approval, but I'm also concerned about losing my job.

A: In place of acting inauthentically to get approval from your boss and others, try experimenting with simply giving acceptance and attention to your boss and others. When we *give* love or approval to others, we are filled with a sense of loving Presence, not when we *get* love or approval from others.

By being very present and giving attention to everything in your experience, including your boss, it's more likely that you'll respond appropriately and with integrity to whatever is happening. Doing this may not guarantee that you keep your job (nothing can), but it will mean you have more integrity, wisdom, strength, acceptance, and compassion available to meet whatever does happen. Whether you stay in this job or end up looking for another, being very present and accepting will make the experience easier and more joyful for you. It will also allow you to be more effective in dealing with people, which can only help either in this job or in finding another.

Giving love can transform all of your experiences, not just your relationships at work. Love is essentially just space (acceptance) and attention (noticing). You don't even have to like whatever you are giving this loving attention to. Just let it be the way it is, as you notice everything about it. It's easiest to try this out with neutral or pleasant objects first. Then when you have the hang of it, try giving space and attention to things and eventually people that are annoying or difficult to be with. In addition, give loving acceptance and attention to yourself and your own reactions to others. You do not need to leave yourself out of the loving awareness, and there may even be important information about the situation that is found in your responses to others.

While it may seem paradoxical, it is in giving love that we are filled with love. When love is flowing from within you, it won't matter as much to you how other people act or react. It's incredibly freeing to discover that you can go ahead and give acceptance and attention to everything you encounter and that will fill you with an authentic sense of loving acceptance. (You can read more about giving love to everyone and everything in "Love Is for Giving," which is included in this book as Appendix 2.)

Love is at the heart and core of our true nature. All the fundamental qualities of our true nature come together as love. Love is the force that connects us and fuels our desire to create, understand, experience, and ultimately merge with everything we experience. Every movement of life is the movement of love. Love is your true nature. Love is what you are.

The Truth in Daily Life: A Talk by Nirmala

An mp3 recording of a talk given in satsang is available to purchasers of this book at:

http://endless-satsang.com/part6mp3

Chapter 7

GRACE

all may have a mind of their own
but thoughts are gifts of grace
touching mind for an instant
like melting snowflakes

every place can be home
but rest is a divine blessing
when effort falls away
like the setting sun

the heart may burn with emptiness
but love comes in waves
smoothing away doubts
like a tide erasing footprints in the sand

From Gifts with No Giver by Nirmala, a free collection of nondual poetry, available at http://endless-satsang.com/free

Invitation to Rest

Satsang is an invitation to rest, not just an invitation to realize, find, or understand yourself. That happens—that's part of it. But the real core and heart of satsang is an invitation to rest, to simply rest as yourself. The value of any spiritual understanding or realization is the degree to which it allows you to just rest as yourself, to just be yourself and let Grace unfold your life.

You don't have to wait until you've had a profound spiritual realization to accept this invitation. In your spiritual journey, you can pull over any time. You don't have to wait for the rest area. Just pull over. Get out of the car, walk around, lay down under a tree, just *be* for a while. Satsang is like a rest area, an ever-present invitation to just simply notice what it's like now, in *this* moment. Take a moment of rest from the journey to understanding or the journey to a better life or the journey to spiritual realization.

Satsang is an invitation to rest now, to rest even if there still is a longing for realization or an impulse to get somewhere. Sometimes the desire is to get somewhere, and sometimes it's to get away from somewhere or to not have the experience you're having. If either of these desires is present, that's fine. You can rest even if these desires or impulses are present. Just because you pull over doesn't mean you won't still have the impulse, the urge, to keep going. So the invitation is to rest with that impulse and take the time to experience it, to actually have the experience you are having, which may include a lot of desire, a lot of hope, or a lot of fear and resistance. What's that like? What happens if you just rest here with all of your hope and your resistance?

It's not that there's anything wrong with inquiring into where to go, how to get something, or how to get rid of something. There's nothing wrong with that kind of inquiry. It's just that satsang is an invitation to a much simpler inquiry, an inquiry into what is already here. You can even inquire into what is already at rest in your being. Even resting isn't something you do. It turns out you don't really have to pull over to rest. What is at rest right now? What is simply *being* right now? Being is being, whether you're wanting to be somewhere else or not, whether you're efforting or not, whether you're resisting or not.

"What do I want?" is a valid question. But more fundamental questions are: "What is already here? What is your existence like right now?" The invitation in satsang is to ask: "What am I right now?" and "What is it like to *be* here?" including any impulse to be somewhere else, because that may be part of what's here. You don't have to pick and choose what parts of your present experience to include. You don't have to do any weeding of your experience or clearing out of the underbrush. You can leave it all there and notice that there's also something here that is at rest.

Probably the last place you would think to look for something at rest is in the impulses, movement, activities, and doing of your life. It may seem like you have to get rid of all your desires and activities before you can rest. But that idea just results in a more subtle list of things to do. Rather, the invitation is to ask who is it that has a to-do list? No matter how many things are crossed off or being added to that list, what are you in all of that? What is this self?

It's not that there's anything wrong with the journey of life or even with spiritual seeking. But somehow along the way, the seeking often acquires so much momentum that we abandon the sense of ourselves. We stop noticing, recognizing, or honoring the fact that we already exist. We become so involved with where we're going and what we need to do that we lose track of what we *are*.

So the invitation is to rest in what you are right now. It's an amazing thing that you exist right now. Whether you are happy or sad, whether you are healthy or sick, whether you are enlightened or not enlightened, you still exist right now. What's that like? What is this that simply exists? You always are. There isn't anything you have to get rid of first to rest in this moment. There isn't anything you have to accomplish first. Every moment is equally worthy of this simple inquiry into what are you.

Every place is a really good place to start resting. There isn't a better place than right here to start resting. Just start where you are, even if you are hurt or overwhelmed or confused or desperate or ecstatic or excited or afraid. All those feelings are fine and very natural. It's normal to feel them, and they are always also an opportunity to rest. What a strange thing it is to consider that even being excited or scared is an opportunity to rest. Every other flavor of experience is equally an opportunity for resting. All experiences are Grace appearing in her endless disguises.

The Flower of Awakening

The following is from the free ebook That Is That *by Nirmala, which is available at http://endless-satsang.com/free*

Consider the miracle of a flower. What is it that causes a plant to flower? Does sunshine? Does lots of water? Or is it good soil? Maybe all of these together? Or is there really something more subtle in the nature of the flower itself that causes it to flower? Is it something in the DNA of the plant? Does that mean the whole process of evolution over eons of time is involved? What other factors might cause the flowering? Does gravity play a part? The season and the temperature? The quality of the light? What about animals that eat the fruit and spread the plant? Or the birds or bees that pollinate the flower? Do they cause the subsequent flowering of the newly established plants? Are there even subtler influences? What about Presence and love? The intention and attention of a gardener? And is the existence of the world of form itself necessary for a plant to flower? What about consciousness? Is there a force that directs the creation and unfolding of all form that is behind the appearance of a rose or a daisy?

What if what causes a flower is a combination of all of the things mentioned? And what if all of these things have to be in the right proportion? Is that proportion different for every species of plant? Some plants need lots of water or light to flower. Others will die with too much water or light. A unique formula is involved in the appearance of the simplest apple blossom and the most complex orchid.

When you consider all these influences and others that weren't mentioned or can't even be known or imagined, then it is truly a miracle when a flower appears. It's impossible to say what causes it to happen with any certainty or completeness. Yet, it's an act of incredible grace whenever all these diverse, subtle, and gross influences come together in just the right way for an iris or a daffodil to open its unique petals to the sky. If you trace all the factors back to all their causes, you find that everything that exists is somehow intimately connected to the cactus flower or dandelion in your front yard. We need a mysterious and powerful word like "Grace" to name this amazing interplay of forces and intelligence. To reduce it to a formula doesn't come close to capturing or describing the vast richness of variables and forces at play. There's no formula complex enough to capture the mystery of a magnolia blossom.

Awakening is a kind of flowering of consciousness. When consciousness expands and opens into a new expression, we call that an awakening. And while there are as many kinds of awakenings as there are flowers, they are all equally mysterious. What is it that causes a child to awaken to the nature of words and language? How does one suddenly know he or she is falling in love? And how does one explain the birth of unconditional or divine love?

What are the causes of the most profound spiritual awakenings, where consciousness suddenly recognizes its true nature? Why does that type of flowering appear in one consciousness today and another one tomorrow? If the formula for a simple petunia is a vastly complex interplay of earthly, human, and even cosmic forces, then imagine how complex the formula is for the unfolding of a human consciousness into full awakeness. The good news is that we can't and don't need to know the totality of the formula for growing petunias, and we can't and don't need to know the formula for spiritual realization. Yet, we can be curious about all the factors involved and even play with them to see what effects, if any, they may have in our own experience of consciousness unfolding.

Sometimes the mysteriousness and unpredictability of the process of awakening leads us to conclude it is all up to Grace or God. And, of course, that is true. But does that mean there's no place in this unfolding for our own actions? Is there a place for spiritual practice? What about meditation, self-inquiry, or studying spiritual texts? What about devotional practices or the transmission of Presence from a great teacher or master? We can easily become disillusioned with these activities because the results can be so unpredictable and varied, and it may seem simpler to avoid the question of their role altogether. Ask any gardener if it works every time to water, weed, and fertilize a plant? Or does a plant sometimes fail to flower no matter how well it is cared for? However, does that mean you never water or fertilize your plants?

At other times, we can be overly convinced that our practice or inquiry will produce the desired results, maybe because it worked for us once or for someone we know. The only problem with spiritual practices is that they occasionally work! Then we think we have the formula and that every time we meditate or ask, "Who am I?" we'll have the same experience of expansion or Oneness. That's like thinking you'll have a bumper crop of marigolds every time you plant them.

There is a middle way between denying the value of spiritual practice and expecting that inquiry, meditation, or devotional practice will, by itself, result in awakening. We can experiment and play with these practices, just as a gardener experiments with different fertilizers or watering patterns. In the end, it is all up to Grace. But what if Grace works through us as well as on us? What if spiritual practice is as much a part of the mystery of existence as anything else?

Maybe we can hold the question of what role inquiry, devotion, effort, surrender, transmission, meditation, gratitude, intention, silencing the mind, studying spiritual books, involvement with a teacher or master, ripeness of the student, karma, grace, and luck play in our awakening with an openness and curiosity instead of needing to define their roles once and for all. The flowering of your consciousness is as unique as every flower, and you are here to discover how it's going to happen uniquely through you.

What is your consciousness like right now? How open is the flower of your awareness? Is it still budding, or has it blossomed? Just as every flower fades and another comes along, what about now? And now? What happens this time when you meditate? What happens now when you inquire, "Who am I?" How does it feel right now to open your heart with gratitude even if nothing much is happening? What impact does reading this or anything else have on you? Every stage of a plant's existence is valuable and even necessary for its flowering. Your experience is always adding to the richness of the unfolding of your consciousness in this moment. May you enjoy the garden of your true nature.

Grace Is All There Is

Q: Can you tell me what Grace is? I'm struggling to understand it.

A: Very simply, Grace is your essence, your true nature. Grace is what you really are, and Grace is all there is. Specifically and practically speaking, Grace is the intelligent, optimizing movement of life. This optimizing force is what unfolds every moment in the direction of greater truth and love and greater functioning and fullness of life. Grace is the nourishing Presence that holds us and supports us in the unfolding of our life. You have experienced Grace directly many times, when things just fell into place or you were touched by a deeper understanding and awareness.

While Grace is obvious in moments when the seemingly miraculous occurs or when a profound opening into the depths of Being happens, Grace also knows when a difficulty or obstacle has the potential to lead to a greater depth of awareness and a fuller expression of our limitless potential. This means that Grace can show up as a flat tire on the way to work or a broken heart or any of the minor and major difficulties we face in everyday life.

In understanding and appreciating Grace, the challenge and the opportunity is to see that Grace is always here and always bringing us the exact experience that is most useful and helpful. Sometimes only in hindsight can we see the Grace in our struggles and suffering, but Grace is always here. Recognizing the Grace in our challenges often allows a challenge to be resolved more naturally and effortlessly, or at least allows us to be at peace with it. The healing of our suffering comes when we see the bigger truth that even suffering is a part of the unfolding of Grace. When you see that there is Grace even in your own problems, then it no longer matters if some difficulty occurs as the situation is no longer as much of an experience of suffering, but just what is happening.

Understanding Grace doesn't require an intellectual grasp of what it is or even insight into how it works. Understanding Grace only requires that you be open and curious about your experience just as it is right now. Are you willing to see Grace as she is appearing right now this very moment? Can you recognize her even if she is artfully disguised as pain or discomfort? Can you open your Heart to the gift she is offering you today?

The understanding doesn't come as some final insight or as an answer to all your questions. The understanding comes as a felt sense of trust that life is safe and good and worthwhile. The understanding comes as the unfolding of life moment to moment. This is the miracle of Grace, touching you in every moment and always as close as your own breath. Because you will never be done discovering all the infinite ways that life and Grace can unfold and express itself, the complete understanding of Grace will take forever. What an adventure and blessing it is to be shown the many dimensions and possibilities of your true nature as intelligent, loving, infinite Grace.

Q: I can see that experiences are neither good nor bad unless I judge them. So basically, I see experiences as neutral and not even benevolent. Things just happen, not toward any greater good. I can hold the concept that all experiences are benevolent and beneficial, but from what I see around me, I'm not sure this is true. How is starvation benevolent or beneficial? When I see horrific cruelty to animals, I can't see any Grace or benevolence. If Grace acts through experiences, it sure chooses some pretty horrific ways to get its point across, and this has hardly led to the mass flowering of enlightenment. If starvation and cruelty were beneficial tools, surely millions would be awakened and awakening by now. To me, life looks more like a mixed bag of tricks and treats without any purpose or meaning.

A: Everything you share is true, and there is still the question of how true. Is it the whole truth? Is it the biggest truth? Is it possible that while all of the hurt, pain, and suffering in this world are real, there is still a bigger truth to this existence? This doesn't mean denying or ignoring suffering or not acting in ways that would relieve or reduce the horror and tragedy that are part of life. But while acknowledging and attempting to alleviate the suffering, you can look for and question the possibility of a greater intelligence and Presence that is also operating in this world and beyond it. A bigger truth than the pain and suffering is the truth that consciousness isn't harmed by anything. Bodies can be harmed and even die, but can consciousness be damaged? I'm inviting you to hold this as an open question, something to be discovered as life unfolds here on earth and also beyond your time here on earth.

Here and now, you can directly discover for yourself the bigger truths. The truth is what opens your Heart and quiets your mind, while a smaller truth contracts your Heart and makes your mind very busy. So check this out for yourself: Does believing that life is a mixed bag with no purpose open your Heart? And what effect does it have on your Heart to hold the possibility that consciousness can't be harmed, and that it has a deeper purpose in life? Which idea gives your Heart more room to breathe and just be? I invite you to explore this capacity of your own Heart to discriminate how true every idea, hope, dream, fear, worry, and intuition is. Truth comes in many different sizes from extremely small to infinitely big, so discrimination is needed to determine how true things are.

In my view, we are both right, and the truths I share and the truths you shared are not contradictory, but complementary. Even if we can't see how these truths fit together, we can at least recognize that there is room for both of them. A bigger truth is not better, just bigger. A smaller truth is not worse, just smaller. You can respond to and include all sizes of truth in your awareness: You can feed the starving, feel intense grief and sadness over unnecessary cruelty and destruction, and also discover the limitless peace and love that are also here in every moment. You can also discover for yourself the depth of your soul that has never been and never will be harmed. And you can see that same depth in the eyes of a starving child if you look deeply enough.

Staying Awake Until Grace Comes

Experiences of your true nature are a movement of your divine nature, or Grace. They aren't something you do. All of the profound experiences of love, peace, and joy that you are blessed with in this life come to you through the intelligence and power of divine Grace.

Since there's nothing you can do to make there be more Grace or more peace, joy, and love in your life, what's left is an opportunity to simply notice more often the Grace that is already here. This noticing is not really a doing or a making something happen. It is also not a non-doing, which is often just the *doing* of inaction. Noticing, inquiring, and paying attention are in between doing and not-doing. Or you could say, noticing is doing something that is already happening. Awareness is already happening, so when you notice something, you are "doing" this awareness that is already here! This paradox is what makes the noticing so powerful, without it necessarily reinforcing the illusion that you are in charge or making things happen.

Action and inaction still occur as a natural part of life. However, do you notice the Grace that is also present and that is present in all your actions and inactions? Grace is all there is. So all you need to do to live more fully in this ever-present love, peace, and joy is to give these things more of your attention. You don't need to make love, peace, and joy happen or create more love, peace, and joy, but you *can* notice them more and more. Can you see the love present even in the movements of the ego? Can you feel the peace that is present in the empty space in the room right now? Can you experience the joy and natural curiosity that is already present in your questions before you find any answers?

Can you also be more fully present to your experience when it seems that Grace is a distant memory? The opportunity is to also notice what appears to be in the way of seeing the peace, joy, and love that are here and to find out what is true about these veils or illusions. Can you see Grace even in the movements of your mind and ego, which seem to hide Grace from view?

You can't live more in this non-personal way because you already live totally in this non-personal way. The only misunderstanding is the idea that your life is somehow personal. The antidote is to see that your human life is already an expression of a supremely profound Grace and divine love. Your life doesn't just flow within you or only as the particular events that you want to experience. It flows through you, everyone, and everything. Grace appears as everything that ever happens.

The recognition of this deeper truth also just happens. Noticing and paying attention simply create a situation where that recognition is noticed when it happens. Effort to make the recognition happen doesn't work, and unfortunately *not* efforting to make it happen doesn't work either. Paying attention doesn't make it happen either, but it does mean that you are paying attention when the recognition spontaneously happens. My favorite metaphor for this is how sometimes you can't remember someone's name, and no matter what you do, you still can't remember that person's name. Then ten minutes later, when you're no longer trying to remember the name, it pops into your mind. Paying attention or noticing is what is required to notice the name when it finally appears. Similarly, you can't make spiritual realization happen, but paying attention means you'll experience it when it comes. A deeper recognition of the love that is always here is a function of Grace itself. Paying attention just means you stay awake until it happens!

The Point of Spiritual Practice: A Talk by Nirmala

An mp3 recording of a talk given in satsang is available to purchasers of this book at:

http://endless-satsang.com/part7mp3

APPENDIX 1: BEYOND NO SELF

The following is from That Is That *by Nirmala, which is a free ebook that is available at http://endless-satsang.com/free*

The spiritual journey is a movement away from over-identification with the body and mind to the rediscovery of our true identity as infinite Being, and this can be two different movements. The first movement is dis-identification with the body and mind. Since identification is just a movement of thought, dis-identification is simply a movement away from thought. The ego identification that we experience most of the time is the result of repeated thoughts about "I," "me," and "mine." That is all there is to it, but while we are thinking these thoughts the sense of self is contained in them. And since most of our self-referencing thoughts are about our body, our thoughts, our feelings, and our desires, the sense of self is usually contained in the body and mind.

Dis-identification from the thought form of the ego can occur whenever there is a deep questioning of the assumption that is present in most of our thoughts that we are the body and the mind. Inquiry using the question, "Who am I?" can naturally weaken the assumption that we are the body and the mind. In fact, any deep questioning of our thoughts and assumptions can loosen our over-identification with thought, since so many of our thoughts aren't very true. Experiences of no thought can also weaken this identification because in the absence of thought, is an absence of identification. We all experience this when we get so caught up in what we are doing that we completely "forget ourselves."

Alternatively, sensing the Presence that is aware of the thoughts can also disentangle us from the tendency to identify with our thoughts. The second movement of the spiritual journey is this recognition, or realization, of our true nature as Presence, or limitless Awareness. It is a wonderful surprise to discover that everything that really matters in life, including peace, joy, and love, is found in this empty Awareness. This emptiness is incredibly full and rich. It has intelligence, strength, and compassion. Whenever we experience a deeper quality of Being, such as clarity, peace, satisfaction, value, happiness, or love, it's coming from this spacious Presence.

The surprising thing is that while these two movements can occur simultaneously, they can also happen apart from each other. When this happens, the movement from ego identification to our essential nature is incomplete. Although it's a profound insight and a huge relief to discover, by examining and questioning our thoughts, that we are not the body or the mind (after all, if I'm not my body, then these aren't my aches and pains; and if I'm not my mind, then these aren't my problems), by itself this insight only reveals our false assumptions, not the truth about who we really are. So it's possible to dissolve the ego by seeing through the mind without actually experiencing our true nature, which is a Heart-centered experience. In a sense, you can wake up out of your mind but not be in your Heart.

When this happens, there is a sense of relief from all the grief caused by over-identification with the body and mind but also often a deep sense of meaninglessness: If *I* don't exist, then what's the point? It doesn't matter anymore what the fictional *I* does or what happens to it. In fact, it feels like nothing matters at all because everything is so clearly an illusion.

When seekers are led or just find their own way to a deep experience of no self, they can then form a new, more subtle belief that this absence of self is all there is. "I'm not my body, I'm not my mind, I don't exist" are seen as the final conclusions. From a purely logical perspective, what more is there to say, since there's no one here to say it or hear it! And while these conclusions are true, they aren't the *whole* truth.

Underlying all the mind's activity is the non-conceptual reality of Being, or our true nature. It is a pure, empty, aware space that is full of the subtle substance of Presence and all of its essential qualities: peace, joy, love, clarity, strength, value, and much more. How can that be—empty space that is full of everything that matters? The mind can't grasp it fully, as Presence exists beyond concepts. And yet, that is what we really are. We experience it with more subtle senses than the physical senses and the mind. We "sense" it by being it. We just are this full, yet empty, Presence.

It is this second movement of realization of Presence that counteracts the belief that since I (as ego) don't exist, therefore nothing exists and everything is an illusion. The realization of Presence, or Essence, gives back to our life a heartfelt sense of meaning and purpose, which becomes a pure expression of the wonder and beauty of this deeper reality. Instead of living a life in service to the ego's wants and needs, we are moved to fulfill the deepest purpose of a human life: to serve and express freedom, joy, beauty, peace and love. By itself, the realization of no self can end up dry and lifeless, but when the Heart opens wide to the greater truth of the true Self, life is anything but dry and lifeless.

The opposite can also occur: Our awareness can move into pure Presence and be filled with a sense of the limitless goodness of our true nature. And while any experience of our true nature does, to some extent, loosen the identification with the limited idea of ourselves that we call the ego, an experience of our true nature by itself doesn't always dissolve the ego completely. Having a profound experience of our true nature doesn't take away our capacity to identify. It doesn't render us incapable of thought. We can still return to thinking of ourselves as a limited self—but one that has now tasted our true nature.

So, after such an experience, if the habit of identification with the body and mind does continue, it may still be necessary to deconstruct the mistaken beliefs related to ego identification. There's a place for inquiring into the false beliefs and assumptions of our identification with the body and mind, and a place for inquiring into the underlying reality. The difference is that inquiry into our true nature isn't a purely mental activity. Because of the subtle nature of Presence, the inquiry has to be subtle and wholehearted. To discover what's really here requires subtlety, patience, persistence, courage, tenderness, compassion, curiosity, and ultimately everything you've got! The momentum of our usual identification with thoughts and physical reality shapes our perception to such a great degree that breaking through to the more subtle dimensions of perception can be a challenge.

It helps to pursue the inquiry into true nature with both the Heart and the body. The mind's view is so easily distorted by belief and conditioning that the experience beneath the shoulders is often a more direct and open doorway into Presence. What are you experiencing right now in your shoulders? In your heart? In your belly? What is the space around your arms and legs like right now? Is there energy flowing in your body right now? Questions like these can direct you to a more fruitful exploration, especially if you ask them with your whole being and not just with your mind.

Appendix 1: Beyond No Self

It is a saving grace that this deeper reality is always present. Sometimes it only touches us in an unguarded moment of deep loss or profound beauty. In the end, there's no escaping from the truth. Illusions come and go, beliefs come and go, but the underlying Presence remains.

To experience Presence, all we have to do is stop believing in our thoughts and sense our being. It is really that simple, although doing this isn't necessarily easy. One of the things that makes experiencing Presence a challenge is the sense of identity we naturally have. Anytime we add something to the statement "I am," as in "I am scared" or "I am a bird watcher," our identity moves into that thought. This is what it means to identify with thought. A thought by itself has little power or significance. But a thought that begins with "I" or "I am" or one that is about me, my possessions, or my experience evokes a sense of identity. It's as if our true nature moves into or tries on the shape and feel of the thought. Dissolving or deconstructing the thoughts that we identify with can free our essential identity from an assumption that it is somehow contained in our body or our mind. Seeing the falseness of those ideas opens the door for our deepest sense of our own existence to move out of the tight confines of our beliefs and ego identifications.

Often when the sense of self is set free from the structures of ego-centered thought, it naturally expands into a full experience of true nature. We call a sudden expansion into true nature like this an awakening, as it seems we have awakened to a whole new reality that is rich and full of joy, peace, and love.

However, then it is possible for the sense of self, or identity, to move into a different belief or an assumption of no self. This happens most often when the focus of a teaching or inquiry is on the negation of false identifications, without a counter-balancing emphasis on the underlying reality of Presence. Some spiritual practices are specifically designed to negate false identifications, such as the practice of seeing that you are not this and not that until nothing is left. Some spiritual teachers and teachings emphasize the non-existence of a separate individual and go on to suggest that not only is the individual not real, but the world and everything in it is also not real.

There is a profound truth in this perspective, as it penetrates and dissolves the usual belief or assumption that the ego, our thoughts, and physical reality are more real than more subtle levels of reality. Even when we have tasted a deeper reality, we often return to an ego-centered perspective because of the momentum of our involvement with the physical and mental realms. Even in the face of profound experiences to the contrary, there's a habit of assuming that our physical body and our beliefs and other thoughts are what is most important, so much so that we think that everything that pops into our heads is important. We even use the argument, "That's what I think" to justify our position, as if thinking something makes it true. Since our most common thought or assumption is the assumption that "I am the body" or "I am my thoughts, feelings, and desires," this pointing to the falseness or incompleteness of those most basic beliefs is vitally important to loosening the grip of the ego.

However, in the absence of the experience of our true nature, there is this danger of the sense of self simply landing on a new belief in no self. The sense of self moves from a limited and painful identification with the mind's idea of who you are to a more open and freeing idea of emptiness and non-existence. While this may be a relief, it can eventually be just as limiting as the original ego identification. When our sense of self has identified with nothingness, emptiness, or no self, we can become stuck there.

This is often reflected in a kind of defensiveness of this new identification: Anytime you are challenged, you deflect the criticism or conflict by retreating more fully into the idea of no self. Or you turn the tables on those challenging you and try to convince them that they don't exist, therefore their concerns aren't valid. This new identification with no self can feel flat, dry, and detached. Life feels like it has no meaning or value. So what was once a helpful and freeing dissolving of limiting structures has become a new fossilized and limiting identity.

Because it is your essential identity or sense of self that moves into or identifies with the concept of emptiness or no self, it is a very convincing new identification. Whenever identity moves into an experience, it doesn't just experience it but actually becomes it to a degree. When your sense of self is firmly planted in the body and egoic mind, it feels like that is who you are. And when, instead of just experiencing emptiness, your identity or sense of self moves fully into emptiness or no self, it also is very convincingly felt as who you are. When you move so fully into identification with something that it no longer feels like an experience but who you really are, the experience becomes more global and convincing.

This is the power of identification to make an egoic thought and the false self, or ego, seem more real than it is. The power of identification can also make the dry emptiness and meaninglessness of no self seem more real. They are both illusions, but it is through identification that illusions are made to seem real. Being or consciousness is ultimately the one that is identifying, and when limitless eternal Being identifies to create illusion, it does a good job of it!

However, no matter how powerful the illusion of the egoic self or no self is when we are identified with it, identification is still simply a movement of thought followed by a movement of our sense of self into that thought. Since thought is always a temporary phenomenon, no identification is ever permanent. In fact, every identification only lasts as long as the thought triggering it. We become "stuck" in identification by repeating a lot of similar thoughts. The sense of an egoic self or no self are both created by a pattern of repeated thoughts that identity moves into.

Because this movement of thought is temporary, there is always, in every moment, the possibility of touching the deeper reality of our true nature. What is even more amazing is when, with repeated experiences of our true nature, our identity, or sense of self, moves into the realm of essential reality. Eventually it becomes obvious that Presence is actually who we are. When our identity moves into our true nature, there is no suffering and no dryness or emptiness. We simply are all of the peace, joy, and love in the universe.

There is nothing you can do to move your identity, or sense of self, into your true nature. Identity isn't something you do; it is what you are. However, the sense of identity follows your awareness, and since you are ultimately everything, it can and will identify with whatever is in your awareness. This is the danger of a teaching that doesn't point to or convey the existence of true nature. If something isn't even talked about or considered, it's much less likely that awareness will notice it and that identity will shift into it. This is why it's important to teach and explore all the qualities of Presence, such as joy, peace, and love, so that awareness begins to touch them and identity eventually shifts to the underlying truth of Being.

A subtle distinction needs to be made between your true identity and the sense of self you have in any moment. Your true identity has and always will be the infinite spaciousness of Being, including all forms, both physical and subtle, and all of the formless emptiness of pure space. But your sense of self is a flexible means for this limitless Being to experience itself from many different perspectives. By having this ability to move in and out of all kinds of experiences and appear to become them by identifying with them, Being gets to try on many different experiences or illusions, from the most contracted and limited to the most expanded and blissful. Without this capacity, Being would be a static existence of infinite potential that is never expressed. By moving its identity into and identifying with the myriad perspectives of limited experience, this potential becomes experienced in form and movement.

So while mis-identification is the root of all your "problems," it isn't and never has been a mistake. Being has very purposefully shifted its identity in and out of infinite apparent selves to try them all on for size. Being stuck in identification is itself an illusion, since all identification is temporary. Every expression of life is an expression of the right way to be, if the right way to be is simply to express our limitless capacity to experience identification and dis-identification, form and formlessness. The deepest, fullest experience of anything is to become it, and that is what Being has been up to all along.

The ultimate freedom is the discovery that it is fine to identify and dis-identify. True freedom demands no limits, not even limits against limitation. Since Being itself is completely free and cannot be harmed, it has been endlessly exploring every possibility of that freedom. This perspective will allow you to hold everything, even the spiritual journey, lightly. The goal is and always has been the journey itself. You can be curious about this whole process of identification with the ego, with no self, and with true nature simply for its own sake. It is a rich and mysterious world of perception and reality that we as consciousness inhabit. Why not taste it all? Life is and has always been this endless movement in and out of identification, in and out of forms and formlessness.

Finally, here is a short fairy tale about Being, which captures some of this freedom in a story:

> *Once upon no time, there was an infinite and eternal Being. Needless to say this was one big Being. Being infinite and eternal meant that no matter where or when it went, there it was. And of course, anything that big was made of empty space, as space is the only thing big enough to be that infinite.*
>
> *While space is a wonderfully low maintenance thing to be, since it can't be harmed, this Being still had a problem: There was no one else. Since it was already everywhere and every-when, there was no place or time for anyone else. It was not a horrible problem, but still there was no one else to talk to, dance with, or play with.*
>
> *What's an infinite Being to do? It can't really just create lesser beings inside of itself as that would not be very interesting to an infinite Being. For a truly infinite and eternal being to create little lesser beings to play with would be like you or me making dolls to play with as an adult. There's nothing wrong with that, but that's not very interesting after a while.*
>
> *Then it had a great idea! Being infinite meant it also had infinite potential, so rather than create lesser beings, it decided to create more infinite beings. At first this would seem impossible since there is the question of where would you put another infinite Being? There already is no space left over once you have one infinite Being. But the great thing about space is that it is completely empty as long as it's pure space or pure potential, so two spaces can actually occupy the same space!*
>
> *That was the solution! So Being created an infinite number of infinite space Beings just like itself. In a sense, Being cloned itself.*

Now, rather than having just a wind-up doll version of a Being to relate to, it had real, fully amazing infinite Beings like itself to relate to.

Even better, it quickly discovered that as long as one of the infinite space Beings stayed "home" as infinite space to hold the endless universes in place, then all of the rest were free to contract into all kinds of shapes and sizes. In fact, all a Being of infinite potential has to do to contract into a different shape or size is think about it, and voila it happens! That's the power of infinite potential!

Now not only could all these infinite Beings hang out as one very big space (which of course really meant hanging out as one Being, since two spaces in the same space are really still just one space), they could also play at contracting into all kinds of lesser expressions of their infinite potential.

Now why would they want to do that? Why would something infinite want to experience being less than its infinite self? Well remember these Beings are not only infinite, but also eternal, and eternity is a very long time! That means they all had a lot of time to kill. What does it matter if you spend a little time experiencing yourself as less than your complete potential, especially if you can do an entire eon standing on your head and still have all the time in the world?

And so Being, as many Beings, was now free to talk, dance, create, and play in all kinds of crazy wonderful ways because now there was someone else to talk, dance, create, and play with. Party time!!!

Ever since, it has been discovering all of the different things it can identify with and temporarily become and all of the truly strange and amazing things it can do once it has become less than itself. Infinite space can't really play soccer or be a super nova or fall in love or have its heart broken or create a new universe or fly a kite when it's expanded into its original nature as infinite space, but if it contracts into a form or expression of itself, then it can do all of that and more!

So that is what it's been up to ever since, and it's really just getting started, since it still has so much time on its hands; the rest of eternity is still a very long time. That is also why it's so amazing to relate to others: because it is never some lesser incomplete being across the table from you. It is always an infinite Being with infinite potential that you are talking to or playing with. No wonder they are so convincing in their role as an apparent separate individual. It is really God playing that role. There are only Gods upon Gods upon Gods being everybody and everything and doing everything that is done! That is what we all are.

Pretty clever solution if you want to have some fun, don't you think?

APPENDIX 2: LOVE IS FOR GIVING

The following is from Living from the Heart *by Nirmala, which is available at http://endless-satsang.com/free*

What is love and where is it found? We search for love and try to get love, and yet it seems like we never get enough. Even when we've found it, it can slip away as time passes. What if there is a source of love that never fades and is always available? What if love is as near and easy as breathing? What if you have been "looking for love in all the wrong places" instead of actually lacking love?

Love is both simpler and more mysterious and subtle than we imagine it to be. Love is simply the spacious, open attention of our awareness, which is the gentlest, kindest, and most intimate force in the world. It touches things without impinging on them. It holds all of our experience but doesn't hold it down or hold it back. And yet, inherent in awareness is a pull to connect and even merge with the object of your awareness.

It's this seemingly contradictory nature of awareness—the completely open and allowing nature of it and its passionate pull to blend with and even become the object of its attention—that gives life its depth and sweetness. There is nothing more satisfying than this delicious dilemma of being both apart from and, at the same time, connected to something you see, hear, or feel.

Awareness is the beginning of all separation. Prior to awareness, there is just oneness or "is-ness," with nothing separate from the oneness that would be able to experience it. With the birth of awareness comes the subtle distinction of two things: that which is aware and the object of awareness. And yet, those two are connected by this mysterious force we are calling awareness, or love.

This flow of awareness and love that connects you to all you experience is the true source of satisfaction and joy. We have all experienced it to some degree. Whenever you fall in love with a person, pet, piece of music, beautiful object, or anything else, you have felt this flow of intimate, connected awareness. Unfortunately, we've been taught to believe that the source of this good feeling was the object of our affection. So we suffered whenever we lost our apparent source. When your lover leaves, your beloved pet dies, the concert ends, or your dream home is repossessed, you feel bereft of that loving, connected feeling.

You Are the Source

But what if you are the source of the awareness that connects you to everything? What if the love you have been seeking has always been right here inside your own Heart? What if it doesn't matter what your awareness touches, but only that awareness is flowing? That would profoundly simplify the search for love. Anything or any experience would be a suitable object for your love.

The sweetness of love is in the flow of awareness itself. The completely allowing openness and freedom you might look for from a perfect lover is already here in your own awareness. It doesn't have to try to be accepting because awareness is, by nature, open and allowing. By itself, awareness can't do anything but touch. It can't push or pull or demand something from or limit the freedom of what it touches. And yet, it is not an aloof, distant observer. It is deeply and intimately connected to the object of awareness. In fact, awareness and the object of awareness come from the same source and are ultimately the same thing.

This connection and intimacy that is natural in awareness is satisfying and fulfilling regardless of the object of awareness. In other words, whatever you are experiencing right now is your true love. Whatever you are experiencing is an opportunity to also experience the depth of your true nature as open, loving awareness. Your true nature is true love. It is the perfect lover you have been seeking, and not only is it always here, but it is who you really are.

You might be thinking, "But wait, I don't feel like I'm in love or loving all the time. Sometimes I feel lonely or angry and cut off from love and satisfaction." So how can it be that love is here, but you don't feel it? Is love really absent in those moments, or is it just limited in its expression and flow? Are there really moments when there is no awareness? Or is there always some awareness, even if it isn't a lot? If there were no awareness, there also would be no problems because awareness is the beginning of separation (the sense of a separate self), and the end of awareness is the end of separation. Practically speaking, without awareness, there can't be loneliness, anger, or anything else. So when you are lonely or angry, there is at least some awareness, although possibly not much.

Even when awareness is contracted and tight, as it often is when you are lonely, angry, sad, hurt, or afraid, it has the same nature as when you are happy and excited. Even a single drop of water is still wet, and even a single drop of awareness is still open and allowing of whatever it is touching.

The only trick to experiencing the open and allowing nature of awareness is to look for it in the actual experience you are having. When your awareness is contracted by judgment or fear, it's not actually touching the object of your judgment or fear.

Instead, it is touching the judgmental or fearful thought you are having. Awareness is completely allowing and open to that thought. That is the definition of awareness: it is the open and allowing recognition of the content of our experience. If awareness is not open to something, then we are not aware of it.

The key to experiencing love is to notice where awareness is flowing right now. That flow of awareness is love, and it's the most satisfying and nourishing thing you can experience. There is naturally a direction to this flow of awareness. It moves from within your being to the objects nearby and the experiences you are having. You can only fully experience this flow of aware love as it moves in that direction.

When someone else is lovingly aware of you (not of their judgments or desires regarding you, but simply of you as you are), you can experience the outer expression of their love. You can see the way they are looking at you, the smile on their face, and their reactions to you. But the awareness of you is arising in them. The love is flowing from them toward you, and so it is filling them with a sense of satisfaction and joy. If you also are to feel satisfaction and joy, it will depend on whether you are experiencing a flow of love toward them. It is your own open awareness that fills you with that sense of connection and appreciation. *You are filled with love when you are giving it to someone or something else.*

Obviously, it's easier to open your Heart and express love when the requirements of your conditioning are being met. When someone who matches your ideal for a lover is attracted to and interested in you, it's especially easy to give him or her the same openness and attention in return. So naturally, when two people are falling in love, they are both feeling the fullness and richness of the free flow of awareness, or love. But the contact each of them has with that love is within themselves. It's their own love and awareness that is filling them up so richly.

This truth—that you are filled with love when you love, rather than when you are loved—can free you from the search for love outside yourself. If you still aren't sure that it is your own love that fills you, think of a time when someone was in love with you, but you weren't in love with him or her. The flow of loving attention toward you wasn't satisfying. In fact, it might have been uncomfortable having someone so interested in you when you weren't feeling the same way.

In contrast, when you are falling in love with someone, it can be rich, exciting, and energizing, even if it isn't reciprocated. In unrequited love, there is an intensity and beauty from the outward flow of love that is filling you in that moment. So despite the disappointment and hurt of not being loved back, you experience a fullness and aliveness as a result of loving the other. In the Renaissance, unrequited love was even seen as an ideal. It's the love flowing out from your own Heart that fills you with joy and satisfaction. The source is within you.

Just One Being

There is just one awareness and one Being behind all the individual awarenesses. The way you can reach that oneness of Being is by experiencing the flow of love from within your being. Paradoxically, the place where you are connected to others is inside your own Heart. You can't really connect to another externally. Even if you used super glue to attach yourself to another person, there would still be a sense of separation in your outer experience, not to mention how hard it might be to disconnect!

On the inside, you are already connected to everyone and everything. The connection is this flow of awareness that is here right now reading these words. It is in the loving nature of awareness that the sense of connection is found, not in the objects of awareness. You are connected to others in the awareness flowing from within you to them. Connection is not found in the flow of awareness and love toward you, as that flow is connected to its source inside the other person.

This is good news! You can experience limitless love no matter what anyone else is doing. The only thing that matters is how much you are loving, not how much you are loved. Right now, you can be filled to overflowing with the incredible sweetness of love, just by giving awareness to anything and everything that is present in your experience. Don't take my word for it; test it out with this exercise:

Exercise: *Allow your awareness to settle on a physical object nearby. Take an extra moment to allow your awareness to fully touch the object. Just for the sake of this experiment, give as much love, appreciation, and acceptance as you can to that object. Then notice another object. As your awareness rests for a moment on that, give it as much love, appreciation, and acceptance as you can.*

Now allow your awareness to notice a sound in your environment. As you listen, give that same loving appreciation to the sound you are hearing.

If you have any difficulty giving love and appreciation to a particular object or sound, try another object or sound. If you pick a more neutral object or sound, it will be easier at first to experience loving something for no particular reason.

Continue allowing your awareness to land on various objects, sounds, colors, tastes, smells, and sensations. With each one, allow as much love and appreciation to flow toward it as you can. Take as long as you like with each experience, and if it's difficult to feel love toward something, just move on. It will get easier to love for no reason as you repeat this exercise.

Now notice other things that may be arising within you: an uncomfortable sensation, a thought, a feeling, or a desire. Take an extra moment to send loving attention toward it. Just for now, you can love each sensation, thought, feeling, or desire that appears within you.

As you get the hang of this, you can just allow your awareness to move naturally to whatever it touches next, either inside or outside of you. Whatever it lands on, give it love and acceptance. Just for a moment, let it be the way it is.

What is it like to give simple awareness and love over and over to things that appear in your experience? How open and full does your Heart feel when you are able to give love in this way? If you come to something that's difficult to love or accept, just notice that it's difficult, and then love that it's difficult right now. You can even take a moment to simply love the way some things are harder to love than others. Then move on to whatever is in awareness next.

Just go ahead and love whatever is in front of you, and in that way be filled with love. It's that simple, if you remember that the essence of love is awareness and space. The ideal lover is someone who gives you lots of space to just be yourself but still connects with you as you are. Awareness is like that. It doesn't limit the object of its awareness, but it makes contact.

You Can't Run Out of Love

You can give this awareness or love freely because awareness is the one thing you can never run out of. No matter how many things you've been aware of today, you still have awareness left for this moment and the next. Awareness is easy to give, and it doesn't cost anything or deplete you in any way. In your Heart, there is a limitless supply of love. Just see if you can give so much attention to something that you end up with no more awareness.

We sometimes withhold love and awareness because we think that true love requires more than this simple, open attention. Our conditioning suggests that love requires things like compromise, sacrifice, and unconditional giving of our time and effort. Perhaps some of these are necessary for a relationship, but not for love.

This is an important distinction, as we often confuse love and relationship. We mistakenly believe that love is dependent on relationship. But if we recognize that the source of love is within us, then relationship can be seen in perspective. Relationships are important, but they aren't as important as love. The experience of this inner flow of love is satisfying, either with or without a relationship. You can experience it with a beautiful object of art in a museum, a moving piece of music, an exciting moment in a sporting activity, or in a deep connection with another person. Love is what makes relationships and everything else worthwhile.

What a rich possibility—that all the love you have ever wanted is available right now, just by giving it to everything you encounter, both within you and in the environment. Love is for giving, not for getting. And the more you give, the more fully it fills your Heart to overflowing.

About the Author

After a lifetime of spiritual seeking, Nirmala met his teacher, Neelam, a devotee of H.W.L. Poonja (Papaji). She convinced Nirmala that seeking wasn't necessary, and after experiencing a profound spiritual awakening in India, he began offering satsang and Nondual Spiritual Mentoring with Neelam's blessing. This tradition of spiritual wisdom has been most profoundly disseminated by Ramana Maharshi, a revered Indian saint, who was Papaji's teacher. Nirmala's perspective was also profoundly expanded by his friend and teacher, Adyashanti.

Nirmala offers a unique vision and a gentle, compassionate approach, which adds to this rich tradition of inquiry into the truth of Being. He is also the author of *Living from the Heart, Meeting the Mystery, Nothing Personal, That Is That,* and *Gifts With No Giver.* He has been offering satsang, or spiritual teaching, throughout the United States and around the world since 1998. He lives in Sedona, Arizona with his wife, Gina Lake.

Watch videos of Nirmala and download free book excerpts and ebooks on his website at

http://endless-satsang.com

Nondual Spiritual Mentoring

Nondual Spiritual Mentoring with Nirmala is available to support you in giving attention and awareness to the more subtle and yet more satisfying inner dimensions of your being. Whether it is for a single spiritual mentoring session or for ongoing one-to-one spiritual guidance, this is an opportunity for you to orient your life more completely toward the true source of peace, joy, and happiness, especially if there is not ongoing satsang or other support available in your location. As a spiritual teacher and spiritual mentor, Nirmala has worked with thousands of individuals and groups around the world to bring people into a direct experience of the spiritual truth of oneness beyond the illusion of separation. He especially enjoys working with individuals in one-to-one sessions because of the greater depth and intimacy possible.

Mentoring sessions with Nirmala are an opportunity for open-ended inquiry. In your session, you can ask any questions, raise any concerns that are meaningful to you, or simply explore your present moment experience, which is a doorway into a deeper reality. Regular weekly, biweekly, or monthly mentoring sessions can be especially transformative. These mentoring sessions are offered over the phone and typically last an hour. For more information or to arrange a session, please visit

http://endless-satsang.com.

Printed in Great Britain
by Amazon